for dear Malcolm.

GAY
LETTERS

on his birthday:

from Eoin
with love.

8: IX: 95.

First published in 1995 by
MARGINALIA PRESS
an imprint of Ippon Books Ltd
55 Long Lane
London
N3 2HY

ISBN
Hardback: 1874572 80 1
Paper back: 1874572 90 9

Design & Production by Susan Homewood

Printed by Redwood Books,
Trowbridge, Wiltshire

GAY
LETTERS

selected & edited
by
JAMES JOLLY
and
ESTELLE KOHLER

Foreword
by
SIR IAN McKELLEN

Marginalia
PRESS

ACKNOWLEDGEMENTS

The editors are grateful to the following: Nicolas Soames, Duncan Steen, Peter Davies for his help and support, Bill Homewood for all his time and care, and not least for translating (from Old French) the second letter of Edward II. Thanks also to Liz Pierce for sub-editing and to Susan Homewood for design and production.

Detailed acknowledgements of copyright material may be found in SOURCES AND BIBLIOGRAPHY on page 171.

(1)

H. M. Prison.
Reading.

Dear Bosie,

After long and fruitless waiting I have determined to write to you myself, as much for your sake as for mine, as I would not like to think that I had passed through two long years of imprisonment without ever having received a single line from you, or any news or message even, except such as gave me pain.

Our ill-fated and most lamentable friendship has ended in ruin and public infamy for me, yet the memory of our ancient affection is often with me, and the thought that loathing, bitterness and contempt should for ever take that place in my heart once held by love is very sad to me: and you yourself will, I think, feel in your heart that to write to me as I lie in the loneliness of prison-life is better than to publish my letters without my permission or to dedicate poems to me unasked, though the world will know nothing of whatever words of grief or passion, of remorse or indifference you may choose to send as your answer or your appeal.

I have no doubt that in this letter in which I have to write of your life and of mine, of the past and of the future, of sweet things changed to bitterness and of bitter things that may be turned into joy, there will be much that will wound your vanity to the quick. If it prove so, read the letter over and over again till it kills your vanity. If you find in it something of which you feel that you are unjustly accused, remember that one should be thankful that there is any fault of which one can be unjustly accused. If there be in it one single passage that brings tears to your eyes, weep as we weep in prison where the day no less than the night is set apart for tears. It is the only thing that can save you. If you go complaining to your mother, as you did with reference to the scorn of you I displayed in my letter to Robbie, so that she may flatter and soothe you back into self-complacency or conceit, you will be completely lost. If you find one false excuse for yourself, you will soon find a hundred, and be just what you were before. Do you still say, as you said to Robbie in your answer, that I "attribute unworthy motives" to you? Ah! you had no motives in life. You had appetites merely. A motive is an intellectual aim. That you were "very young" when our friendship began? Your defect was not that you knew so little about life, but

The opening page of 'De Profundis', Oscar Wilde's moving letter to Lord Alfred Douglas, written in Wilde's cell at H.M. Prison, Reading, on grim blue prison notepaper

From page 39 of 'De Profundis', showing Wilde's second thoughts and re-workings

CONTENTS

SIR IAN McKELLEN

FOREWORD

BY SIR IAN MCKELLEN

Dear Reader,

Judging by my mail these days, I am not alone in writing fewer letters than I used to. Circulars, invitations and bills are a sort of correspondence and some strangers need answering; but, picture postcards aside, it is increasingly rare for friends to pick up a pen and, when we want to keep in touch, the telephone is more handy. Instantaneous communication is the convenient, modern way, thanks to the everyday magic with which we can harness satellite, time and space to an intimate, international call.

About the fax, I am less sure. A facsimile by definition is not the real thing. Pressing the 'start' button and watching the paper slide through and out can be exciting, with the prospect of an immediate response. Yet when the reply comes, if it comes, looking just like every other limply curling message, there is none of the unique personality of a letter lying seductively on the front door mat. With care, ink and even pencil can be kept forever but the print of faxes fades. Soon, no doubt, I shall succumb to the modem but I am not enthusiastic about messages that flicker across a screen.

Certainly technology is no way for lovers to correspond. It denies that overwhelming thrill of the familiar handwriting on the unopened envelope. How do you seal a fax with a loving kiss? Once your letter falls down inside the pillar-box, the waiting is exquisitely painful. 'If he gets it tomorrow or, considering the distance, maybe the day after, will he write back straightaway and will I get it soon, soon, soon?' Even when the first post fails to deliver, or the second, disappointment is tempered by the masochistic delight of joy postponed. Tomorrow it may come. Then, of course, you pick up the phone. 'Did you get my letter?'

Erasmus, too, nervously wondered why his beloved had not written: 'What shall I guess to be the reason?' Great thinkers are not impervious to common complaining. Many of the other letters in this collection ring familiar bells of jealousy and insecurity. 'What care and anxiety, nay what fear had you spared me, if you had written to me only once or twice on your journey' the lovelorn 54-year-old Hubert Languet writes to the 18-year-old Philip Sidney. Then comes the reassuring reply, that ends 'May God grant you long life for my sake'. Languet must have read that over and over.

The title 'Gay Letters' will mislead any reader who is hoping for intimate revelations about the particular problems and delights of homosexual desire through the ages. Without the editors' notes you couldn't always guess the writers' particular sexuality. This is neither a prosetylising, nor an academic study relating to the rights of lesbians and gay men to be treated equally with the rest of society. Subsequent anthologies can do that but they may well want to reprint the couple of explicit letters which are included here. Estelle Kohler and James Jolly have cast a wide net and revealed what the world at large is only just beginning to appreciate, that the daily preoccupations of most gay people coincide with those of the rest of the population. Are we not, after all, any more queer than other folk? Is there no such thing as an especially gay sensibility?

Identifying yourself as gay, in private and in public, is a welcome phenomenon but too modern to apply to most of the other letters herein. Indeed some of the writers might want to sue; on grounds of what? defamation? exaggeration? bewilderment? When it comes to outing the dead, I'm all for it.

My favourite contribution is the only fictional one, not just because Armistead Maupin and his lover Terry Anderson showed me the way out of the closet but because in Michael 'Mouse' Tolliver's 'Letter to Mama' (page 169), we can read the best 'gay letter' yet.

Ian McKellen
London, May 1995

xii

INTRODUCTION

'The Laws of God, the laws of man
He may keep, that will and can.
Not I.'
A. E. Housman

'Dear Bosie, After long and fruitless waiting I have determined to write to you myself, as much for your sake as for mine...' So starts Oscar Wilde's *De Profundis*, his letter to Lord Alfred Douglas, his one-time lover, from H. M. Prison, Reading. It is one of the most famous 'gay letters', indeed it must be one of the most famous letters of this century – written, no doubt, with posterity in mind, but at the same time obviously from the heart. Oscar Wilde has assumed a unique rôle in literary and political history, not because of his extraordinary gifts (that rôle was guaranteed anyway) but for the appalling treatment he received at the hands of the British Establishment. 'De Profundis' might be a useful subtitle to a good many of the letters collected in this volume. The love that dare not speak its name may have had to endure a covert existence, but in print it has flourished over the centuries.

The word 'homosexual' means 'same sex'. It was coined in the nineteenth century by German psychologists. In America the first recorded public use of the word 'gay', in the context of sexuality, was in the 1939 film *Bringing up Baby*, when Gary Grant, wearing a dress, says he has 'gone gay'; but it is certain that as a subcultural euphemism the word has been around a lot longer than that. It might have been derived from the nineteenth-century slang of London, New York and Paris bachelor society or, as has been mischievously suggested by etymologists, from the French Provençal word 'gai', traditionally a euphemism for prostitute, or from any number of other sources – but wherever it comes from it is a friendly word.

The late John Boswell, in his book *The Marriage of Likeness*, wrote that the early Christian Church tolerated homosexuality and actually conducted marriage services for homosexual couples. Through the centuries, however, hostility towards men who love men, and women who love women, has often been fomented by fundamentalist Christians; for example, during the 500 years of the Crusades the traditional tolerance of homosexual behaviour within Islamic cultures was a target for the evangelistic conquerors. In the last 200 years in England and America there have been countless examples of recriminatory homophobia in the name of the Christian God; more recently in America, the 'born-again' Christians, under the banner of The Moral Majority, have used selective passages from the Bible to attack gay men and women as 'sinful'. The Old Testament story of Sodom and Gomorrah (Book of Genesis) has always been especially useful to these arguments. There are countless examples of discrimination against gay people today; for example, at the time of writing, the age of consent in Britain for mutual homosexual acts has not been lowered to match that for heterosexual acts; it is illegal in the military in both Britain and America 'to practise homosexuality'; gay men and women in public life are forced, by the threat of exposure in a scandal-hungry press, to be especially discreet in their behaviour; gay men in particular are considered to be a security risk owing to the prejudicial assumption that they are promiscuous and might be the subjects of blackmail. The influential psychologist Sigmund Freud suggested that boys became homosexual in the absence of strong fatherhood, which added fuel to nineteenth-century attitudes towards gay men and continues to affect current thinking; more recently AIDS has added to these prejudices and has been used as a weapon in hostile propaganda. In this light it is not surprising that most treasuries and anthologies exclude gay correspondence, or that loving correspondence between gay men has mainly been discreet; this is especially true of those letters written during intolerant times. Nevertheless, this book contains many wonderful exchanges where caution has been thrown to the wind.

However, though there are a good number of letters celebrating love – J. R. Ackerley's beautifully candid, and strangely 'innocent', reports of erotic encounters in Japan and Greece, Rupert Brooke's first (and only?) gay experience, Thomas Gray's devotion to Richard West – this book is primarily a glimpse into the lives and experiences of many gay men. Countless influential men have been gay and every letter has been chosen either for its intrinsic historical interest or for its quality of writing. It is not an exhaustive selection; executors and literary trustees are still defensive in certain quarters, but we hope it is representative.

Above all *Gay Letters* is presented not as a political or defensive work, but as a tribute to man's capacity for affection, and his humanity towards man.

James Jolly
Estelle Kohler
May 1995

EMPEROR HADRIAN
AD 76 – 138

Hadrian succeeded his guardian, the Emperor Trajan, in AD 117, and ruled until his death. Trajan's wife, Empress Plotina, arranged Hadrian's marriage to Vibia Sabina (believed to have been only twelve years old). The marriage was not a great success. Hadrian preferred the company of a beautiful eighteen-year-old Greek youth, Antinous – but she often accompanied him on his famous travels, taking with her a close friend, possibly her lover, the poetess Julia Balbilla.

Antinous is known to have travelled to Egypt with Hadrian in AD 130, where tragically he drowned in the River Nile. It was said that Hadrian 'wept for him like a woman', and that 'there was a star, which he said he himself saw, and knew to be that of Antinous. He harkened gladly to his servants, as they told him that the star was in truth begotten of the soul of Antinous, and then for the first time appeared to men'.

Heartbroken, Hadrian named an Egyptian city after him: Antino, or Antinopolis, founded on the bank of the Nile at the very spot where his lover died. Subsequently Hadrian commissioned statues and busts of his lover, and established the Antinous Games in his honour.

Here, before Antinous's death, Hadrian writes to his brother-in-law, the Consul Lucius Julius Ursus Servianus:

So you praise Egypt, my very dear Servianus! I know the land from top to bottom, a fickle, tricky land, blown about by every wind of rumour. In it the worshippers of Serapis are Christians, and those who call themselves Bishops of Christ pay their vows to Serapis. There is no ruler of a Jewish synagogue there, no Samaritan, no Christian presbyter, who is not an astrologer, a soothsayer, a quack. Whenever the patriarch himself comes to Egypt he is made to worship Serapis by some and Christ by others.

The men are a most seditious, addle-pated, riotous crew. The town is rich, prosperous, productive. There is not an idle person in it. Some are glass makers, others paper manufacturers, others linen weavers. Every one seems to have some trade and is supposed to have one. The gouty are busy; the blind are energetic; not even hands crippled by gout keep the victim from an active life. They all of them have one and the same God, Money. Christians adore Him, Jews worship Him, all the Gentiles give Him adoration. It is a pity that the town has not got better morals. For its productivity certainly makes it deserve the reputation which its very size gives it, that of the First Town in Egypt.

I have made the town every possible concession. I restored its old privileges to it, and I gave them new ones so bountifully that while I was actually staying there they paid me thanks! No sooner was my back turned than they began saying many things against my son Verus – and what they have said about Antinous I think you know. My one wish for them is that they may have to eat their own fowls. How they fatten these I blush to repeat.

I am sending you some many-coloured drinking cups, which the priest of the temple presented to me; consecrated they are specially to you and to my sister. Please use them for holiday feasts. But be careful that our friend Africanus does not indulge too freely with them.

Hadrian is, of course, most remembered for 'Hadrian's Wall', a monumental construction built in AD 121–2 from Tyne to Solway, like a necklace across Britain, to separate the Barbarians in the North from the Romans in the South.

ALEXIUS COMNENUS
1081 – 1118

Towards the end of the Dark Ages there was a growth in hostility towards homosexuality – perhaps with the increase in organised broadcasting of political and religious attitudes.
Alexius Comnenus writes to Robert II (made Count of Flanders in 1087):

To the noble and glorious Count Robert of Flanders and to all rulers of all realms, both lay and clerical, who are devoted to the Christian faith, the emperor of Constantinople sends greetings and peace in Our Lord Jesus Christ and His Father and the Holy Spirit.

O incomparable count, great defender of the faith, it is my desire to bring to your attention the extent to which the most holy empire of the Christian Greeks is fiercely beset every day by the Pincinnatti [Patzinaks?] and Turks, and how it is ceaselessly preyed upon and despoiled, and how massacres and unspeakable murders and outrages against Christians are perpetrated. But since the evils committed are so many and, as we said, so unspeakable, we shall mention but a few, which are nevertheless horrible to hear and disturb the very air in which they are spoken.

For they circumcise Christian boys and youths over the baptismal fonts of Christian churches and spill the blood of circumcision right into the baptismal fonts and compel them to urinate over them, afterward leading them violently around the church and forcing them to blaspheme the name of the Holy Trinity. Those who are unwilling they torture in various ways and finally murder. When they capture noble women and their daughters, they abuse them sexually in turns, like animals. Some, while they are wickedly defiling the maidens, place the mothers facing, constraining them to sing evil and lewd songs while they work their evil. We read of a similar act perpetrated in ancient times against the people of God, whom they mocked after humiliating them in various ways by demanding, 'Sing us one of the songs of Sion!' [Ps. 136:3, Vulgate].

Likewise, while defiling the daughters, they compel the mothers to sing wicked songs; the mothers' voices must, we imagine, produce more laments than songs, as it is written regarding the death of the holy innocents: 'In Rama was there a voice heard, lamentation, and weeping, and great mourning, Rachel weeping for the children, and would not be comforted, because they are not' *[Matt. 2.18]*. The mothers of the innocents represented by the figure of Rachel could not be consoled for the death of their children, but they take consolation regarding the salvation of their souls. These mothers, however, so much the worse, have no consolation whatever, since their daughters perish in both body and soul.

But what next? We pass on to worse yet. They have degraded by sodomising them men of every age, and rank – boys, adolescents, young men, old men, nobles, servants, and, what is worse and more wicked, clerics and monks, and even – alas and for shame! something which from the beginning of time has never been spoken or heard of – bishops! They have already killed one bishop with this nefarious sin.

They have polluted and ruined the holy places in innumerable ways and threaten even worse things. In the face of all this, who would not weep – Who would not be moved? Who would not shudder? Who would not pray? Nearly the entire territory from Jerusalem to Greece, and all of Greece with its upper regions (Cappadocia the Greater and Lesser, Phrygia and Bithynia and Phrygia the Lesser), and many other areas as far as Thrace – too many to mention here – have all been invaded by them, and hardly anything remains except Constantinople, which they threaten soon to take from us unless we are speedily relieved by the help of God and the faithful Latin Christians...

These few among countless evils wrought by this most impious race we have mentioned and written down for you, the count of Flanders and a lover of the Christian faith. The rest we pass over as too unpleasant to be read. For the sake of the name of God and the piety of all those who uphold the Christian faith, we therefore implore you to lead

4

here to help us and all Greek Christians every faithful soldier of Christ you can obtain in your lands, great, small, or middling, that they might struggle for the salvation of their souls to free the kingdom of the Greeks, just as in past years they have liberated, to some extent, Galicia and other western kingdoms from the yoke of the unbelievers. For although I am emperor, no remedy remains to me, nor do I know where to turn next, but I am, rather, constantly fleeing from the Turks and Pinemaci [sic: Patzinaks?] and am reduced to waiting in a single city for their imminent arrival. And since I prefer to be subject to you, the Latins, rather than have Constantinople taken by them, you should fight courageously and with all your strength so that you might receive in bliss a glorious and indescribable reward in heaven. It is better that you should have Constantinople than the pagans, since in it are preserved the most precious remains of the Lord: the pillar to which He was bound, the whip with which He was flogged, the scarlet robe with which He was clothed, the crown of thorns with which He was crowned, the reed He held in His hands instead of a scepter, the robe taken from Him at the cross, the greater part of the wood of the cross on which He was crucified, the nails used to crucify Him, the linens found in the sepulcher after the resurrection, the twelve baskets of the crumbs of the five loaves and two fishes, the head of Saint John the Baptist with the hair and beard intact, the remains of bodies of many of the innocents, of several prophets, of apostles, of martyrs (most notably that of Saint Stephen, the first martyr), and confessors and virgins, too many to be named here individually. All of these things the Christians rather than pagans ought to possess, and it will be a great boon to all Christians if they are kept, but a shame and a judgment on them if they are lost...

Act therefore while you have time, lest you lose the kingdom of the Christians and, what is worse, the sepulcher of the Lord, and so that you may earn a reward rather than a punishment hereafter. Amen.

POPE HONORIUS III
died 1227

A hundred years later, Pope Honorius III shows rather more humanity in this letter to the Archbishop of Lund (now Denmark):

February 4, 1227

We have received a petition from you requesting that we deign to provide mercifully for the fact that numerous subjects of yours, clerics and laymen, frequently engage in prohibited sexual relations, not only with persons related to them but also by having sinful intercourse with dumb animals and by that sin which should neither be named nor committed, on account of which the Lord condemned to destruction Sodom and Gomorrah; and that some of these on account of the length and dangers of the journey, others on account of shame, would rather die in these sins than appear before us on such charges.

Therefore, since divine mercy is greater than human perverseness and since it is better to count on the generosity of God than to despair because of the magnitude of a particular sin, we order you herewith to reprimand, exhort, and threaten such sinners and then to assign them, with patience and good judgment, a salutary penance, using moderation in its devising, so that neither does undue leniency prompt audacity to sin, nor does unreasonable severity inspire despair.

Despite Pope Honorius and other humanitarians, by the early thirteenth century in Europe, homosexual acts were punished by execution.

EDWARD II
1284 – 1327

Young Prince Edward, heir to the throne, liked to gather a favourite court of young men around him, to the irritation and finally great anger of his father. Here, young Edward reluctantly carries out his father's orders:

12 July 1305
Chartham

Edward etc. to Robert the Parker, his bailiff of Langley, greeting.

Because our lord the King has charged us to turn out all those who have dwelt at Little London, so that none may dwell there, but the place be kept as it was in the time of our dear lady and mother, whom God assoil; we bid you turn out all those who have remained behind there, if any there are, and in particular Sir Thomas the chaplain, for the King has so commanded us; and cause the place to be kept in the manner aforesaid.

Prince Edward seems to have been incorrigible. In the following letter, translated from his imperfect French (the courtly language of the time), Edward solicits the help of his sister Elizabeth to soften his father's attitudes, particularly with regard to his beloved foster brother Piers Gaveston from Gascony:

Edward etc. to his very dear Sister the lady Elizabeth, Countess of Holland, of Hereford and of Essex: greetings and warm Commendations.

Be assured of our earnest Wishes for the good Health of our Lord the King our Father and that of my lady the Queen our Mother, and that of Yourself. As for Ourselves, we are pleased to report to you of our sound Health at this, the time of writing.

On the matter of the two excellent Yeomen-courtiers granted to us by the graciousness of the King, and whom we housed near to us, that is to say Johan de Haustede and Johan de Weston, we pray and entreat you with all our Hearts to beg my lady the Queen our dear Mother to plead with the King to grant us yet two more Yeomen-courtiers to live near us, that is to say Gilbert de Clare and Piers de Gavastone.

For if we were granted either these two, or the continued use of the others above named, we should be relieved greatly of the Anguish which we have endured, and still endure from day to day, following the orders and wishes of our Lord the King.

Dearest Sister, may the Lord keep you Safe. Written thus under our Private Seal,

Windsor Park
4th. August

Eventually his father banished Gaveston to France, where he stayed until the old king died in 1307. The Prince, now King Edward II, immediately recalled his lover to London. Pressure on the new king to marry, and to consolidate Anglo-French relations, led to his wedding in January 1308 to Isabella, daughter of Philip IV ('The Fair') of France. Edward conferred land and power on Gaveston, who was subsequently executed on Blacklow Hill by the powerful Barons of England, who were jealous of Gaveston, and wished to restrict the authority of the young king.

After Gaveston's death, Edward took a new lover: Hugh le Despenser the Younger, from a powerful landed family. Queen Isabella and her lover Roger Mortimer of Wigmore, in league with the Barons, pursued the couple, exposed them and caused their capture at Berkeley Castle. Hugh le Dispenser's genitals were cut off and burnt publicly, before he was decapitated; Edward was killed by the application of a red-hot poker which was thrust up through his anus into his intestines.

LEONARDO DA VINCI
1452 – 1519

Leonardo da Vinci is thought of today as one of the most brilliant men in history. He combined a fertile scientific and technical mind (e.g. scale drawings of flying machines) with extraordinary and influential abilities as a sculptor and painter (e.g. his great painting The Last Supper*). When he was twenty-four years old, da Vinci and three friends narrowly escaped punishment for associating with a boy prostitute. In his life he was twice arrested for sodomy; his sexual partners are known to have included Francesco Melzi, Andrea Salaino, Cesare da Sesto and Guiliana Boltraffio.*

Here, seeking patronage to develop his many ideas, the great artist and inventor writes to 'The Tyrant of Milan', Lodovicio Sforza:

Most Illustrious Lord, Having now sufficiently considered the specimens of all those who proclaim themselves skilled contrivers of instruments of war, and that the invention and operations of the said instruments are nothing different from those in common use: I shall endeavour, without prejudice to anyone else, to explain myself to your Excellency, showing your Lordship my secrets, and then offering them to your best pleasure and approbation to work with effect at opportune moments on all those things which, in part, shall be briefly noted below.

❧ I have a sort of extremely light and strong bridges, adapted to be most easily carried, and with them you may pursue, and at any time flee from the enemy; and others, secure and indestructible by fire and battle, easy and convenient to lift and place. Also methods of burning and destroying those of the enemy.

❧ I know how, when a place is besieged, to take the water out of the trenches, and make endless variety of bridges, and covered ways and ladders, and other machines pertaining to such expeditions.

❧ Item. If, by reason of the height of the banks, or the strength of the place and its position, it is impossible, when besieging a place, to avail oneself of the plan of bombardment, I have methods for destroying every rock or other fortress, even if it were founded on a rock, &c.

❦ Again, I have kinds of mortars; most convenient and easy to carry; and with these I can fling small stones almost resembling a storm; and with the smoke of these cause great terror to the enemy, to his great detriment and confusion.

❦ And if the fight should be at sea I have kinds of many machines most efficient for offence and defence; and vessels which will resist the attack of the largest guns and powder and fumes.

❦ Item. I have means by secret and tortuous mines and ways, made without noise, to reach a designated [spot], even if it were needed to pass under a trench or a river.

❦ Item. I will make covered chariots, safe and unattackable, which, entering among the enemy with their artillery, there is no body of men so great but they would break them. And behind these, infantry could follow quite unhurt and without any hindrance.

❦ Item. In case of need I will make big guns, mortars, and light ordnance of fine and useful forms, out of the common type.

❦ Where the operation of bombardment might fail, I would contrive catapults, mangonels, *trabocchi*, and other machines of marvellous efficacy and not in common use. And in short, according to the variety of cases, I can contrive various and endless means of offence and defence.

❦ In time of peace I believe I can give perfect satisfaction and to the equal of any other in architecture and the composition of buildings public and private; and in guiding water from one place to another.

Item. I can carry out sculpture in marble, bronze, or clay, and also I can do in painting whatever may be done, as well as any other, be he who he may.

❦ Again, the bronze horse may be taken in hand, which is to be to the immortal glory and eternal honour of the prince your father of happy memory, and of the illustrious house of Sforza.

And if any of the above-named things seem to any one to be impossible or not feasible, I am most ready to make the experiment in your park, or in whatever place may please your Excellency – to whom I commend myself with the utmost humility, &c.

ERASMUS
1466 – 1536

Desiderius Erasmus is sometimes described as the father of the art of letter-writing. A great humanist and communicator, he relished the development of the printing press. Forced into the monastic life by his guardians on the death of his parents, he wrote letters to fellow monk Servetas Roger of Rotterdam. It is possible that the constraint of silence, or partial silence, led to the volume of correspondence between the two men. He really loved Servetas, once confessing: 'I have become yours so completely that you have left me naught of myself. You know my pusillanimity, which, when it has no one on whom to lean and rest, makes me so desperate that life becomes a burden.'

Here he writes two ardent letters to his friend...

Erasmus to Servatius

1492

What are you doing, my Servatius? for I suspect you are doing something great, which prevents your fulfilling your promise to me, You pledged yourself to send me a letter very soon; and see what a great interval has passed, and you neither write nor speak. What shall I guess to be the reason? You must certainly be either too busy or too idle; I suspect both, and that you are living in that leisure, than which nothing is more busy. For a state of desire implies leisure, since love is the passion of a vacant mind. You will therefore do what will please me and be of use to yourself, if you interrupt that leisure, and write to me without any delay. For the rest treat me with confidence, and you will be no more afraid of my conscience than your own. Speak with me about everything as with yourself. That will be what I should wish. Farewell.

Erasmus to Servatius Roterodamus

I should write more frequently to you, very dearest Servatius, if I knew for certain that you would not be more fatigued by reading my letters than I by writing them. And your comfort is so dear to me, that I had rather be tortured by what gives you rest, than fatigue you by what gives me pleasure. But since lovers find nothing so distressing as not to be allowed to meet one another, and we very rarely have that in our power, I cannot forego the opportunity of bidding this letter find its way to you in my stead. How I wish it may be some time our fortune to have no further need of letters, but to be able to meet face to face as often as we please. That joy is denied us; I cannot think of it without tears; but am I therefore to be deprived of all intercourse with you? So suspicious are those that love, I sometimes seem to see, I know not what, – that you do not often think of me, or have even quite forgotten me. My wish would be, if it were possible, that you should care for me as much as I do for you, and be as much pained by the love of me, as I am continually tormented by the want of you. Farewell.

Erasmus eventually left the monastery and accepted employment as tutor to Robert Fisher and William Blount (the 4th. Lord Mountjoy), wealthy young Englishmen sent to Paris for their intellectual and academic betterment. Erasmus developed strong feelings for Mountjoy, expressed in this letter to Robert Fisher...

London, 5 December *[1499]*

To Robert Fisher, Englishman, abiding in Italy, greetings:

I hesitated not a little to write to you, beloved Robert, not that I feared lest so great a sunderance in time and place had worn away anything of your affection towards me, but because you are in a country where even the house-walls are more learned and more eloquent than are our men here, so that what is here reckoned polished, fine and delectable cannot there appear anything but crude, mean and insipid. Wherefore your England assuredly expects you to return not merely very learned in the law but also equally eloquent in both the Greek and the Latin tongues. You would have seen me also there long since, had not my friend Mountjoy carried me off to his country when I was already packed for the journey into Italy. Whither indeed shall I not follow a youth so polite, so kindly, so lovable? I swear I would follow him even into Hades. You indeed had most handsomely commended him and, in a word, precisely delineated him; but believe me, he every day surpasses both your commendation and my opinion of him.

But you ask how England pleases me. If you have any confidence in me, dear Robert, I would have you believe me when I say that I have never yet liked anything so well. I have found here a climate as delightful as it is wholesome; and moreover so much humane learning, not of the outworn, commonplace sort, but the profound, accurate, ancient Greek and Latin learning, that I now scarcely miss Italy, but for the sight of it. When I listen to my friend Colet, I seem to hear Plato himself. Who would not marvel at the perfection of encyclopaedic learning in Grocyn? What could be keener or nobler or nicer than Linacre's judgement? What has Nature ever fashioned gentler or sweeter or happier than the character of Thomas More? But why should I catalogue the rest? It is marvellous how thick upon the ground the harvest of ancient literature is here everywhere flowering forth: all the more should you hasten your return hither. Your friend's affection and remembrance of you is so strong that he speaks of none so often or so gladly. Farewell. Written in haste in London on the 5th of December.

MICHELANGELO BUONNAROTI
1475 – 1564

The painter Michelangelo Buonarroti is most remembered for his extraordinary work on the ceiling of the Sistine Chapel in Rome. His main patrons were the wealthy Medici family and the Pope. His greatest love was a Roman nobleman, Tommaso de' Cavalieri, whom he met in about 1532. De' Cavalieri commissioned many important works from Michelangelo, including 'Titus' and 'Gannymede'.

To Messer Tommaso de' Cavalieri in Rome.

Rome, 1 January 1533.

Very inconsiderately, I presumed to write to your Lordship and make the first move as if I had to in response to something from you; later on I realised my error all the more as I read and savoured your welcome reply. Rather than seeming to behave like a new-born child, as you write, you seem to have been on this earth a thousand times before. And I would feel as if I had never been born or had died in disgrace with heaven and earth, had I not come to believe from your letter that your Lordship would gladly accept some of my works.

This has caused me great astonishment but equal pleasure. And if it is true that you feel inwardly the way you write to me openly, as regards your opinion of my works, then if one of them happens to please you as I hope it will, it must be through my good fortune rather than merit. I shall write no more, in case I tire you. Many things I could say remain unpenned; but our friend Pierantonio, who I know can supply what I leave out, will furnish them by word of mouth.

It is right to tell the recipient the gifts one is sending him, but for good reason I am not doing so in this letter.

[unsigned]

Michelangelo wrote beautiful poems for his lover...

If one chaste love, if one God-given piety,
if one same fortune by two lovers dared,
if one the grief but two the pain is shared,
if one will rules two hearts whose souls agree,
if bodies doubled set one spirit free
and both to heaven rise on quick wings paired;
if love's fire in two self-same souls has flared

14

from one thrust of one dart's trajectory;
if loving one another they spurn self
by mutual pleasure, zest and certain aim
which speeds them both to where they want to go:
if this were true a thousand fold, its wealth
would be a hundreth of the love I claim
is ours, which disdain only could bring love.

Writing of de Cavalieri to his friend Friar Sebastiano del Piombo, Michelangelo wrote: 'I beg you, if you see him, to remember me to him a thousand times. And when you write to me, tell me something about him so that I can bring him to mind, for if he faded from memory I am sure I should immediately fall down dead.' Gay lovers, of course, were unable to live together openly, which often led to a feeling of insecurity; Cavalieri sometimes needed reassurance...

To Messer Tommaso de' Cavalieri in Rome.

Florence, 28 July 1533

My dear Lord. – If I did not think that I had convinced you of my very great, indeed my boundless love for you, I would not have thought strange, nor marvelled at, the fear you show in your letter that since I have not written to you, I might have forgotten you. But it is neither unusual nor surprising, since so many things end at cross purposes, that our friendship too might go wrong; and what your Lordship says to me, I would have said to you.

But perhaps you did this to try me or to rekindle a greater flame in me, if it were possible. Be that as it may, I know for sure that I'll forget your name the day I forget the food I live on; indeed, I could sooner forget my food, which sadly nourishes only the body, than your name, which nourishes body and soul, and fills both with such sweetness that I can feel no pain nor fear of death while my mind remembers it. Imagine in what a happy state I would be, if my eye also had its share.

[unsigned]

Michelangelo was a big-hearted and affectionate man. He once wrote: 'You must know that I am, of all men that were ever born, the most inclined to love persons. Whenever I behold someone who possesses any talent or liveliness of mind, or displays any excellence in action or grace of body, I am impelled to fall in love with him. I give myself up to him so entirely that I no longer possess myself, but am wholly his.'

15

GIOVANNI ANTONIO DE BAZZI
1477 – 1549

Bazzi took the nickname 'Sodoma'. The possible reasons are in dispute: i) 'So doma' – 'I am a trainer of horses', or ii) a corruption of another family name, or iii) a corruption of 'sodomy'. It is likely that, in some witty punning style of his own, there is truth in all three. Born in Vercelli in Piedmont, he was a wild, erratic genius of a painter. Surrounding himself with handsome and gay young men, he was soon separated from his bride. At twenty-three he settled in Siena, where he painted his greatest work (e.g. 'Saint Sebastian', 'The Deposition from the Cross', 'Christ Scourged'). The monks at nearby Monte Oliveto nicknamed him, not 'Sodoma', but 'The Mad-cap' – on account of his gaudy and unconventional dress-sense.

Like his contemporary da Vinci, he was forced to seek patronage...

> To the Most Illustrious Lord Francesco de Gonzaga, Marquis.
> To Mantua to his Most Honourable Lord – to Mantua.

Most illustrious Lord, the Lord most honoured by me, Health. – Some days ago, when passing through Siena, on his way to Rome, Signor Aloysius, the brother and relative of Your most Illustrious Lordship, deigning to come to my room, and going through the garden at his leisure, I told him that I had a wish that you should have something of my work as a memorial of my duty. He told me that to make a picture of the *Madonna with her Infant and S. Francis* would be most agreeable to you. I would much prefer to know if you have any other desire, and in such case, God willing, I will come and visit your Illustrious Lordship, and bring with me the said picture. I had made a Lucretia for Your Illustrious Lordship, but on my way to present it, it was seen in Florence by his Magnificence Giuliano, and I was compelled to leave it with him. I pray Your Ill. Lordship will certainly deign a very small reply to let me know His wishes, and I am always ready to please Him, to whom may God give happiness for a long period.

> E.D.V.S.,
> 3rd May, 1518.
> Io Antonius Sodona *[sic]*,
> Knight of Siena *[Eques Senis]*

16

PIETRO ARETINO
1492 – 1556

Born illegitimately into poverty in Arezzo, Tuscany, from which town he took his name, Pietro was neglected as a child. However, brilliantly self-educated, he became a satirist and dramatist. He made his name with a series of ripe sonnets on the subject of positions for sexual intercourse, illustrated famously by the painter Guilio Romano.

He writes from Venice to his friend Sodoma (q.v.):

Venice, August 1545

To Sodona [sic]

I in opening the letter that you have sent to me, and reading your name beside my own, felt even to my vitals, as if we were embracing each other in real fact with that cordial loving affection, with which we used to embrace when in Rome and at the house of Agostino Chigi, with so much delight, that we should have been tormented had any said that we were even one hour apart. But in the revolutions of life men wander so much, for which reason this man and that man, these and those, one and another, are transported by chances to live in other places that they never thought of seeing. That is the case with my cavalier, a thousand times dear to me, a thousand times honoured, a thousand times gallant. Be certain that you have never faded from my memory, that there in fact you will never die, but ever become young again, as you would wish, in order that I might make us both very young again. But even on this head I say that, even though we were grown old in years, are not our thoughts ever young? What has one to do with the worth of wealth if it is of no other use than to consume the soul of him who possesses it with the misery of anxious thought, so that he enjoys it the less the more he accumulates it? I myself have spent in this city an amount of treasure that even a Prince who found it would seem to have enough. And if any one justly reproves me it pleases me the more to be thought a liberal soul, inasmuch as that is not the reputation, that I hope to leave of myself to the ages that will come after us. Truly we shall live out the term of life fixed by God; thanking Him in the meantime for His mercy in preserving one in life. Whilst so many of our acquaintances are below ground, you have not given up your brush, nor I my pen. Since we have become famous in the arts of painting and writing, Christ may even grant that we may meet again also one day; for which I implore His Goodness that it may be soon. This juncture we await the fortune of the cards.

17

SIR PHILIP SIDNEY
1554 – 1586

Sidney was the perfect Renaissance gentleman – a poet, scholar, soldier, courtier and statesman. His works included Arcadia, The Defence of Poesie *and* An Apologie of Poesie. *As a young man he formed strong attachments to writers Fulke Greville (who became Baron Brook and was also a friend of Francis Bacon q.v.) and Edward Dyer. The young men discussed metre and verse with the great Edmund Spenser (1552?–1599), whose 'The Shepheardes Calender' was dedicated to Sidney.*

In 1572 Sidney received permission from Queen Elizabeth to travel abroad to learn foreign languages. In Paris he witnessed the St. Bartholomew's Day massacre of the Huguenots. The eighteen-year-old scholar fled to Germany with a close friend: the fifty-four-year-old Hubert Languet, a passionate Huguenot. Sidney continued his travels alone. Languet confessed to spending nights sighing over a portrait of Sidney, painted by the great Veronese. In Italy, Sidney received a stream of letters from the lovesick Languet, who worried constantly and jealously for his safety.

HUBERT LANGUET TO PHILIP SIDNEY

What care and anxiety, nay what fear had you spared me, if you had written to me only once or twice on your journey! I did not desire a laboured letter, only a word or two, as, 'this day we arrived here in safety', or the like. You remember how earnestly I begged this of you when you were leaving me. But you will say 'it matters little to you whether you hear or not: when I arrive at Padua or Venice, then I will write to you'. You might have done both, and if you had, I should have thought myself greatly obliged to you. However I would rather suppose that you have met no one to whom you could trust a letter for me, than either that you disregard your promises, or that your affection for me has begun to fail. That it was strong when you left me, I knew by the tears that hardly suffered you to say farewell. I forgive you this crime, and every other which you shall henceforth commit against me, if you will only be careful not to let your thrift for learning and acquiring information, lead you into danger. You remember how often and how solemnly you have promised me to be cautious.

If you fail in this I shall charge you with a breach of the contract that is between us, and you will be forced to confess that you have broken the terms of our friendship.

To offend *me* is of little consequence, but reflect how grievously you would be sinning against your excellent Father, who has placed all his hopes in you, and who being now in the flower of life, expects to see the full harvest of those virtues, which your character promises so largely to produce... But enough of such grave discourse.

I send you an epistle of Pietro Bizarro of Perugia, that you may have before your eyes his surpassing elegance, and make it your model. You will now perceive how unwisely you English acted in not appreciating all his excellence, and not treating it with the respect it deserves. You judged yourselves unworthy of immortality, which he surely would have bestowed on you by his eloquence, if you had known how to use the fortunate opportunity of earning the good will of such a man. *[Bizarro was a man of learning but frustrated by a slow-moving career in England, he moved abroad.]* How much better we Saxons have done. We have shown more judgement in an hour than you in fifteen long years. We saw at once how to gain his favour, and did not lose the chance. Show me one of your countrymen of whom he thinks so highly, as of the person to whom this letter is addressed, and from whom I stole it, for your amusement and gratification. Take care to use it discreetly, and do not put your hand in the wasps nest, and so give me trouble. I will give you leave to cull a few flowers from it, which will serve for the adornment of your letter if you should ever write to the author. He certainly deserves to be painted in his own colours. I hope he will do so.

Farewell, and greet your people from me.

Vienna, 19th Nov. 1573

PHILIP SIDNEY TO HUBERT LANGUET

Your letter of the 4th Dec. arrived yesterday. It brings me another instance of your singular affections for me, which suffer all suspicions to be removed by one short note. If the King's inauguration [King of Poland] is to take place so soon, it is impossible I should be there; but if it should be put off for a month or two, then if it please God I will surely come. I am sorry that various engagements so hamper me, that I must be absent from a place where there is so much to be seen and learnt. But however it may turn out now in the spring I shall make the tour of all that country with the noble count of Hannau, who tells me that he too intends to leave Italy and go to Poland, Bohemia, and your own Saxony. And then, my very dear Languet, I shall see you, and one conversation with you would give me more delight, than all the magnificent magnificences of all these magnificoes.

Meantime I shall stay here for a fortnight, and pass the rest of my time at Padua. At present I am learning the sphere [astronomy] and a little music. My pen I only practise when I write to you; but in truth I begin to find that by writing ill I only learn to write ill, and therefore I wish you would give me some rules for improving my style, and at the same time you may send me those other admonitions which you said you had put off till I should come to you; for I am sure that you will never exhaust your stock of counsel, and that my blunders will give ample scope for your lectures.

I wish you would send me Plutarch works in French, if they are to be bought in Vienna; I would gladly give five times their value for them, and you will be able to send them no doubt by the hand of some trader. There is one thing more which I have often wished to ask of you, but shame always prevented me; however, as Cicero says 'a letter doth not blush', I have a very strong desire to possess your history of the Polish election, which you were once good enough to show me. I pray and beseech you either to send it to me now, or at least when you write again, to pledge me your word that you will give it me when we meet in Germany, when you must add something else of yours by way of interest.

May God grant you long life for my sake.

Farewell, wholly yours,

Ph. Sidney

Venice 19th December, 1573

Once back in England, Sidney met Penelope Devereux. There was pressure on them to marry, but Sidney avoided the liaison. He did, however, make her the 'Stella' of his Astrophel and Stella *sonnet cycle. In 1583 he married the fourteen-year-old Frances Walsingham. Always desirous of active military service he fought in Holland in 1586, dying in Arnhem from a bullet wound in the thigh. His lifetime friends Dyer and Greville (Brook) were very affected by the news. Sir Edward Dyer wrote an elegy expressing his great sadness at the loss of his friend. As for Fulke Greville Brook, he wrote a biography of Sidney. In 1628 Brook was stabbed to death by his manservant and on his tomb the following was engraved: 'Servant to Queen Elizabeth, Counsellor to King James, and Friend of Sir Philip Sidney'.*

ANTHONY BACON
1558 – 1601

The brother of Francis Bacon (q.v.), Anthony visited France when he was twenty-five, where he met Thomas Lawson. Lawson became a lover and lifetime friend. Bacon was arrested in France on a charge of sodomy, though Lawson was not implicated. A certain Barth'lemy Sore, formerly a servant of Bacon's, testified that 'Monsieur Bacon was a bugger'. Bacon appealed to his friend Henri of Navarre, the future King Henri IV of France, who wrote the following letter appealing for clemency:

To Monsieur de Scorbiac, King's Councillor,
Château de Verlhaguet, Montauban

I hear that Monsieur Bacon is appealing to my Council against a sentence given against him by the Seneschal of Quercy at the bench in Montauban. I write now desiring you to bring his right of appeal promptly before the judge and have it granted as expeditiously as possible. The merit of those to whom he belongs is great. We owe many obligations to the Queen, his sovereign; he is also himself strongly to be recommended. He will know how to repay us in kind for mercy shown to him, and we ourselves are told by God to have care for the strangers in our midst, to safeguard their rights, and to see they win justice, and furthermore in the situation in which we find ourselves at present it is as well to show leniency, nor is it reasonable to use all the formalities and harshness of French justice towards them. I am assured of your prudence, good judgement, and fairness in these matters and that you will bring reason to bear upon them. It is not my intention to say more on the subject, except to assure you of my good wishes and to pray the Creator to hold you, Monsieur de Scorbiac, in His Holy care.

From La Rochelle, this twenty-third of September, 1586,
Your entire good and affectionate friend,
'Henri'

As a result of Henri's intervention, charges were dropped and Anthony Bacon was released from custody. Anthony Bacon returned to England, where rooms were prepared for him by his brilliant brother Francis at Gray's Inn. Anthony, like his celebrated brother, was a great intellect and moved in high society. An agent for Queen Elizabeth I, he gave political and religious intelligence to State Secretary Sir Francis Walsingham. Bacon was plagued by ill-health, particularly gout; this certainly interfered with his career, and he never quite found position in the court, despite his reputation.

When young men, he and Francis received stern reproof and injunction from their formidable mother Lady Bacon…

…That you are returned at length I am right glad. God bless it to us both. But when I heard withal that Lawson, whom I fore-suspected, stole hence unto you, to serve his own turn as heretofore; how welcome that could be to your long-grieved mother, judge you. I can hardly say whether your gout or his company are the worse tidings. I have entertained this gentleman, Mr Faunt, to do so much kindness for me as to journey towards you, because your brother is preparing your lodging at Gray's Inn very carefully for you. An honest gentleman, but one that feareth God indeed, and wise withal…

This one counsel your Christian and natural mother doth give you before the Lord, that above all worldly respects you carry yourself ever at your first coming as one that doth unfeignedly profess the true religion, and are not afraid to testify to the same by hearing and delighting in those religious exercises of the sincerer sort, be they French or English. Courtesy is necessary, but too common familiarity in talking and words is very unprofitable, and not without hurt-taking, *ut nunc sunt tempora.* Remember you have no father. And you have little enough, if not too little, regarded your kind and simple mother's wholesome advice from time to time…

Let not Lawson, that fox, be acquainted with my letters… He commonly opened underminingly all letters sent to you from Council or friends. I know it, and you may too much, if God open your eyes as I trust he will. Send it back, to be sure, by Mr Faunt sealed; but he will pry and prattle. So fare you well, and the Lord bless you and keep you forever.

Your mother, A. Bacon.

I trust you, with your servants, use prayer twice a day, having been where reformation is. Omit not for any. Your brother is too negligent herein.

Lady Bacon had no time at all for the company her sons kept. Francis's friend Henry Percy, came in for particular censure. Lady Bacon writes to Anthony with her worries about Francis:

I pity your brother yet as long as he pities not himself but keepeth that bloody Percy as I told him then, yea, as a coach companion and bed companion, a proud profane costly fellow, whose being about him I verily perceive the Lord God doth mislike, and doth less bless your brother in credit and otherwise in his health.

Henry Percy was in fact a dear friend and was still with Francis at his death in 1626. Here is more advice from the anxious Lady Bacon, this time for Anthony:

My man said he heard you rose at three of the clock.

I thought that was not well. So suddenly from bedding much to rise so early; newly out of your diet. Be wise and godly too, and discern what is good and what not for your health. I like not your lending your coach yet to any lord or lady. If you once begin, you shall hardly end. Be wary of suppers late or full. Procure rest in convenient time. It helpeth much to digestion. I verily think your brother's weak stomach to digest hath been much caused and confirmed by untimely going to bed, and then musing *nescio quid* when he should sleep, and then in consequent by late rising and long lying in bed; whereby his men are made slothful and himself continueth sickly. But my sons haste not to hearken to their mother's good counsel in time to prevent.

You must be tender with keeping in your bed so continually. The gout is named *pulmonarius morbus* because it liketh softness and ease. Good son, call upon God to take patiently his correction, and using ordinary good means have comfort and hope yet of better, and endure it as you may with some travel of body more than heretofore. You eat late and sleep little and very late, both enemies to a sound and short recovery. Make not your body by violent and incessant putting in physics, and by practices unmeet, unable to serve God, your prince and country. Make not night day, and day night, by disorder, discoursing and watching, to greater undoing both mind and body.

Despite their mother's advice, the Bacon boys carried on as before.

Anthony, almost forty and, as usual, in poor health, writes to Dr. Barker of Shrewsbury:

Good Mr Barker,

Having understood first by my servant Mainwaring, then by mine ancient special good friend your kinsman Mr Richard Barker, that God of his goodness had moved and disposed your heart, though otherwise a stranger unto me, to employ your best skill and experience to reintegrate my health, or at the least to ease my much pain, I can but render you most hearty thanks for your free goodwill and friendly offer, the performance whereof with your good leave I will be bold earnestly to request by your repair hither.

I will shortly set down certain particulars by way of advertisement to prepare your consultation and advice thereupon.

My late father was much troubled both to the gout and the stone and consequently myself by birth subject hereunto. My complexion sanguine, my constitution of body even from my youth sickly and rheumatic, having been at 14 years of age in danger of losing both mine eyes. Then began to be made a piste of physic. At 27 I travelled into France where having remained 7 years I wrenched my right foot, which outward mischance finding my body otherwise indisposed began to draw down the rheum that way, which, little by little, did so encroach upon me as at the last it grew to a running gout, which held me in my shoulder, mine arm and my hand, otherwise in my knee and my foot, in which state I have continued these seven years, sometimes more, sometimes less pained, and yet not lost, God be thanked, the use of any limb nor have gotten any formed knottiness, but rather a stiffness and weakness in my joints.

The rage of my gout, considering my years being towards 40, is nothing fiery nor red hot, but bringeth with it a swelling and dissolution of my sinews. It takes me by fits as well in the summer as winter, specially if I take never so little cold it removeth often from one place to another very suddenly. My diet is not offensive. My stomach weak and subject to wind. My head free from all headache but exceeding

moist and fruitful in defluctions at this part. My body hath been evacuated both by light purifyings or late vomits.

Thus, sir, have I been bold to confess myself unto you, even from my
cradle to this time, for the state of my body, and will only add this one
thing, without ostentation, God knoweth, but in truth for your right
information, that I have never been troubled with any kind of *leues
veneria*, nor committed any act to occasion it, for the which modesty I
have by some physicians been rather censured than commended,
noting my *abundantia seminis*. And so, good Master Barker, committing
the consideration thereof to your good meaning, knowledge and
experience, I commend myself most heartily unto you, and you to
God's safe protection.

Your entire loving friend,

'A.B.'

*Francis and Anthony were dedicated to male company, though Francis
married eleven-year-old Alice Barnham (1592–1650) in 1603. There were no
children. Lady Bacon writes sadly of her longing for grandchildren...*

God bless you with needful health inward and outward... You
purge still. Me thinketh it should make nature neither to work digestion nor strength, being so long still pulled. What custom of physic
hath done in you God knows...

Look to your health and may God bless you with a good marriage
for your comfort.

Have you no hope of posterity? Only my children counted in the
world unworthy their father's care for and providing for them. Barley
and Pinner, if you had kept them, would have been above 95 marks a
year to you. Do not, I pray you, make yourself a by-word both here
and to such as are but your half-friends, by so selling to your great
lack and encumbrance to this house. Young sons in latter times are
blessed posterity, and it would be well used for them. I should have
been happy to have seen children's childer, but France spoiled me
and mine.

FRANCIS BACON
1561 – 1626

Francis Bacon was classicist, linguist, scholar, philosopher, metaphysical scientist, writer, lawyer and politician; he is even believed by a few dedicated and vociferous admirers of our time to have written all the plays of William Shakespeare. Their evidence is fun, but far-fetched; however, he was certainly one of the most impressive men that ever lived. Late in life he fell in love with a young man called Tobie Matthews, who visited him at Gorhambury, near St. Albans...

Sir,

I have been too long a debtor to you for a letter, and especially for such a letter, the words whereof were delivered by your hand, as if it had been in old gold. For it was not possible for entire affection to be more generously and effectually expressed. I can but return thanks to you; or rather indeed such an answer as may better be of thoughts than words. As for that which may concern myself, I hope God hath ordained me some small time, whereby I may redeem the loss of much. Your company was ever of contentment to me, and your absence of grief: but now it is of grief upon grief. I beseech you therefore make haste hither, where you shall meet with as good a welcome as your own heart can wish.

In 1621, Francis Bacon's enemies accused him, then in the highest office of Lord Chancellor of England, of bribery and corruption. He pleaded guilty, was fined £40,000 and imprisoned. Curiously, after four days he was acquitted and released summarily. Towards the end of his life he wrote an essay on Friendship: De Amicitia, *to commemorate his precious times with Tobie Matthews...*

Good Mr. Matthew,

It is not for nothing that I have deferred my essay *De Amicitià*, whereby it hath expected the proof of your great friendship towards me. Whatsoever the event be (wherein I depend upon God, who ordaineth the effect, the instrument, all) yet your incessant thinking of me, without loss of a moment of time, or a hint of occasion, or a circumstance of endeavour, or a stroke of a pulse, in demonstration of love and affection to me, doth infinitely tie me to you.

The rest tomorrow, for I hope to lie at London; ever being
Your most affectionate and assured friend.
Secrecy I need not recommend.

JAMES I OF ENGLAND AND VI OF SCOTLAND
1566 – 1625

The son of Mary, Queen of Scots and Lord Darnley, James married Anne of Denmark in 1589 and became King of England in 1603. His journey on horseback from Edinburgh to the Coronation in London took thirty-two days, and during it he was not an impressive sight: 'A little fat personage, with large wandering eyes; a bonnet cast by chance upon his head, and sticking on as best it could; his legs too thin for his weight; his clothes so thickly padded out as to resist a dagger-stroke, of which he was in continual dread, that he looked more like a vast seal than a man; a flabby, foolish mouth, widened for the freer extrusion of remarkably broad Scotch – and all these surmounting a horse saddled after the manner of an arm-chair, with appliances for the rider's support, in spite of which his Majesty not infrequently managed to tumble most ungracefully to the ground.' He was certainly original. He would address a courtier as 'My little pork', or the Secretary of State as 'My little beagle' or 'My little wiffe-waffe'.

True to a perennial Royal tradition, James's marriage was a sham, and his favourites at court wielded greater influence than his wife. Here, James writes to one of these: Robert Carr, Earl of Somerset. The letter is an exercise in damage-limitation. Evidently frightened of scandal, the King seeks to protect his reputation and position by use of subtle threats and blackmail...

[Early 1615]

First I take God, the searcher of all hearts, to record that in all this time past of idle talk I never knew nor could out of any observation of mine find any appearance of any such court faction as ye have apprehended; and so far was I ever from overseeing or indirectly feeding of it (if I had apprehended it) as I protest to God I would have run upon it with my feet, as upon fire, to have extinguished it if I could have seen any sparkle of it. As for your informations, ye daily told me so many lies of myself that were reported unto you as I confess I gave the less credit to your reporters in other things since ye could not be an eyewitness of it yourself. Next I take the same God to record that never man of any degree did directly or indirectly let fall unto me anything that might be interpreted for the lessening of your credit with me – or that

28

one man should not rule all, or that no man's dependence should be but upon the King, or any such like phrase, which if I had ever found, then would I have bestirred myself as became both so great a king and so infinitely loving a master. Thirdly, as God shall save me, I meant not in the letter I wrote unto you to be sparing in the least jot of uttering my affection towards you as far as yourself could require, my differing from your form in that point being only to follow my own style, which I thought the comeliest: so as, then, having delivered my mind as fully to May [Sir Humphrey May] as ye could have wished, having written this letter, having quite turned my countenance from 'Grahme' [Sir John Graham, Gentleman of the Privy Chamber] (the like whereof I never did to any man without a known offence). I having received your nephew in my bedchamber, [a bastard kinsman of Robert Carr] the fashion thereof being done in a needless bravery of the Queen, I did surely expect that this idle talk would wear out like the Pope's cursing, especially seeing my own heart knew it to be without a ground.

For I am far from thinking of any possibility of any man ever to come within many degrees of your trust with me, as I must ingenuously confess ye have deserved more trust and confidence of me than ever man did: in secrecy above all flesh, in feeling and unpartial respect, as well to my honour in every degree as to my profit. And all this without respect either to kin or ally or your nearest or dearest friend whatsomever, nay immovable in one hair that might concern me against the whole world. And in those points I confess I never saw any come towards your merit: I mean in the points of an inwardly trusty friend and servant.

But as a piece of ground cannot be so fertile but if, either by the own natural rankness or evil manuring thereof, it become also fertile of strong and noisome weeds, it then proves useless and altogether unprofitable: even so these before rehearsed worthy and rare parts and merits of yours have been of long time, but especially of late since this strange frenzy took you, so powdered and mixed with strange streams of unquietness, passion, fury, and insolent pride, and (which is worst of all) with a settled kind of induced obstinacy as it chokes and obscures all these excellent and good parts that God hath bestowed upon you. For although I confess the greatness of that trust and privacy betwixt us will very well allow unto you an infinitely great liberty and freedom of speech unto me, yea even to rebuke me more sharply and bitterly than ever my master durst do, yet to invent a new art of railing upon me, nay to borrow the tongue of the devil that cannot come within the compass of any liberty of friendship.

And do not deceive yourself with that conceit that I allowed you that sort of licentious freedom till of late. For, as upon the one part it is true ye never passed all limits therein till of late, so, upon the other, I bore (God Almighty knows) with these passions of yours of old, dissembling my grief thereat only in hope that time and experience would reclaim and abate that heat which I thought to wear you out of by a long-suffering patience and many gentle admonitions. But the circumstances joined to the [same?] made them relish ten times worse to my taste than otherwise they would have done if they had only remained in *puris naturalibus* [*in stark nudity*] of passions. For first, being uttered as unseasonable hours and so bereaving me of my rest, ye was so far from condemning your own indiscretion therein as, by the contrary, it seemed ye did it of purpose to grieve and vex me. Next, your fiery boutades were coupled with a continual dogged sullen behaviour towards me, especially shortly after my fall [*James fell from his horse*] though I gave you a far contrary proof after your fall [*Robert Carr fell from his horse, and was visited by the King*] and in all the times of your other diseases. Thirdly, in all your dealing with me ye have many times uttered a kind of distrust of the honesty of my friendship towards you. And fourthly, which is worst of all and worse than any other thing that can be imagined, ye have in many of your mad fits done what you can [*to?*] persuade me that ye mean not so much to hold me by love hereafter as by awe, and that ye have me so far in your reverence as that I dare not offend you or resist your appetites. I leave out of this reckoning your long creeping back and withdrawing yourself from lying in my chamber, notwithstanding my many hundred times earnest soliciting you to the contrary, accounting that but as a point of unkindness. Now whether all your great parts and merits be not accompanied with a sour and distasteful sauce, yourself shall be judge.

Consider likewise of the difference of the things that ye lay to my charge and that I lay to yours. Here is not 'he said' and 'she said', no conjectural presumptions, nor things gathered out of outward appearance. I charge you with nothing but things directly acted or spoken to myself. I wish at [sic] God therefore, and I shall both pray for it and hope it, that ye may make good use of this little mirror of yourself which herein I present unto you. It is not like Sir Walter Raleigh's description of the kings that he hates, whomof he speaketh nothing but evil, for this lays plainly and honestly before you both your best and worst parts.

To conclude then this discourse, proceeding from the infinite grief of a deeply wounded heart, I protest in the presence of the Almighty God that I have borne this grief within me to the uttermost of my ability; and as never grief since my birth seized so heavily upon me, so have I borne it as long as possibly I can. Neither can I bear it longer without committing an unpardonable sin against God in consuming myself wilfully, and not only myself but in perilling thereby not only the good estate of my own people but even the estate of religion through all Christendom, which almost wholly under God lies now upon my shoulders. Be not the occasion of the hastening of his death, through grief, who was not only your creator under God but hath many a time prayed for you, which I never did for no subject alive but for you. But the lightening my heart of this burden is not now the only cause that makes me press you indelayedly to ease my grief, for your own furious assaults of me at unseasonable hours hath now made it known to so many that ye have been in some cross discourse with me as there must be some exterior signs of the amendment of your behaviour towards me. These observations have been made and collected upon your long being with me at unseasonable hours, loud speaking on both parts, and their observation of my sadness after your parting, and want of rest.

What shall be the best remedy for this I will tell you by tongue. But for the easing of my inward and consuming grief, all I crave is that in all the words and actions of your life ye may ever make it appear to me that ye never think to hold grip of me but out of mere love, and not one hair by fear. Consider that I am a freeman, if I were not a King. Remember that all your being, except your breathing and soul, is from me. I told you twice or thrice that ye might lead me by the heart and not by the nose. I cannot deal honestly if I deal not plainly with you. If ever I find that ye think to retain me by one sparkle of fear, all the violence of my love will in that instant be changed in[to] as violent a hatred. God is my judge my love hath been infinite towards you; and the only strength of my affection towards you hath made me bear with these things in you and bridle my passions to the uttermost of my ability. Let me be met then with your entire heart, but softened with humility. Let me never apprehend that ye disdain my person and undervalue my qualities (nor let it not appear that any part of your former affection is cooled towards me). A king may slack a part of his affection towards his servant upon the party's default and yet love him; but a servant cannot do so to his master but his master must hate him. Hold me thus by the heart, ye may build upon my favour as upon a rock that never shall fail you, that never shall weary to give new demonstrations of my affection towards you; nay, that shall never suffer any to rise in any degree of my favour except they may acknowledge and thank you as a furtherer of it and that I may be persuaded in my heart that they love and honour you for my sake, not that any living ever shall come to the twentie[th] degree of your favour. For although your good and heartily humble behaviour may wash quite out of my heart your bypast errors, yet shall I never pardon myself but shall carry that cross to the grave with me, for raising a man so high as might make one to presume to pierce my ears with such speeches.

To make an end then of this unpleasing discourse, think never to value yourself to me of any other merits so much as by love and heartily humble obedience. It hath ever been my common answer to any that would plead for favour to a Puritan minister by reason of his rare gifts, that I had rather have a conformable man with but ordinary parts than the rarest men in the world that will not be obedient, for that leaven of pride sours the whole loaf. What can or ever could thus trouble your mind? For the exterior to the world, what can any servants expect of their prince but countenance or reward? Do not all court graces and place come through your office as Chamberlain, and rewards through your father-in-law's that is Treasurer? Do not ye two, as it were, hedge in all the court with a manner of necessity to depend upon you? And have ye not besides your own infinite privacy with me, together with the main offices you possess, your nephew in my bedchamber besides another far more active than he in court practices? And have you not one of your newest kinsmen, that loves not to be idle, in my son's bedchamber? With this should ye have silenced these news-bringers and makers of frays. For no other thing is left behind but my heart, which ye have neither cause to doubt nor, if it did need, could they counsel or advise you how to help.

Thus have I now set down unto you what I would say if I were to make my testament. It lies in your hand to make of me what you please, either the best master and truest friend or, if you force me once to call you ingrate, which the God of Heaven forbid, no so great earthly plague can light upon you. In a word, ye may procure me to delight to give daily more and more demonstrations of my favours towards you, if the fault be not in yourself.

Somerset was eventually succeeded in the King's favour by young George Villiers, whom James created Duke of Buckingham. Like Carr before him, he was hated for his presumption. The King is known to have been careless about matters of personal hygiene, but he wore Buckingham's picture 'on a blue ribbon under my wash-coat'.

Buckingham married Lady Katherine (Kate) Manners. The night after the wedding he received the following letter from King James:

To George Villiers, Marquess of Buckingham

17 May 1620

My only sweet and dear child,

Thy dear dad sends thee his blessing this morning and also to his daughter. The Lord of Heaven send you a sweet and blithe wakening, all kind of comfort in your sanctified bed, and bless the fruits thereof that I may have sweet bedchamber boys to play me with, and this is my daily prayer, sweet heart. When thou rises, keep thee from importunity of people that may trouble thy mind, that at meeting I may see thy white teeth shine upon me, and so bear me comfortable company in my journey. And so God bless thee, hoping thou will not forget to read over again my former letter.

James R.

To George Villiers, Marquess of Buckingham

1622

My only sweet and dear child,

I am now so miserable a coward, as I do nothing but weep and mourn; for I protest to God, I rode this afternoon a great way in the park without speaking to anybody, and the tears trickling down my cheeks, as now they do, that I can scarcely see to write. But, alas! what shall I do at our parting? The only small comfort that I can have will be to pry into thy defects with the eye of an enemy, and of every mote to make a mountain; and so harden my heart against thy absence. But this little malice is like jealousy, proceeding from a sweet root; but in one point in overcometh it, for, as it proceeds from love, so it cannot but end in love.

Sweet heart! be earnest with Kate to come and meet thee at new Hall [*Royal residence in Essex*] within eight or ten days after this. Cast thee to be here tomorrow, as near as about two in the afternoon as thou canst, and come galloping hither. Remember thy picture, and suffer none of the Council to come here for God's sake! Write not a word again, and let no creature see this letter. The Lord of heaven and earth bless thee, and my sweet daughter, and my sweet little grandchild, [*godchild*] and all thy blessed family, and send thee a happier return both now and thou knowest when to thy dear dad and Christian gossip.

James R.

George Villiers, Duke of Buckingham

December 1623

My only sweet and dear child,

Notwithstanding of your desiring me not to write yesterday, yet had I written in the evening if, at my coming out of the park, such a drowsiness had come upon me as I was forced to sit and sleep in my chair half an hour. And yet I cannot content myself without sending you this present, praying God that I may have a joyful and comfortable meeting with you and we may make at this Christmas a new marriage ever to be kept hereafter; for, God so love me, as I desire only to live in this world for your sake, and that I had rather live banished in any part of the earth with you than live a sorrowful widow's life without you. And so God bless you, my sweet child and wife, and grant that ye may ever be a comfort to your dad and husband.

James R.

Shortly after this letter was written, King James died. The Duke of Buckingham was immediately charged with causing the King's death by poisoning. Buckingham was acquitted but, never a popular man anyway, he lost the last vestiges of authority in the court from that time.

JOHN WINTHROP
1588 – 1649

Winthrop was the first Governor of Massachusetts, and a leading Puritan. He sailed to America in the Arabella in March, 1630. In 1640 he wrote to his friend Sir William Springe...

I loved you truely before I could think that you took any notice of me: but now I embrace you and rest in your love: and delight to solace my first thoughts in these sweet affections of so deare a friend. The apprehension of your love and worth together hath overcome my heart, and removed the veil of modestye, that I must needes tell you, my soule is knitt to you, as the soule of Jonathan to David: were I now with you, I should bedewe that sweet bosome with the tears of affection: O what a pinche will it be to me, to parte with such a freinde! if any Embleme may expresse our Condition in heaven, it is this Communion in love: I could, (nay I shall) envye the happinesse of your deare brother Barnardiston that he shall enjoye what I desire nay (I will once let love drive me into an extacye) I must repine at the felicyty of that good Lady (to whom in all love and due respecte I desire to be remembered) as one that should have more parte than my selfe in that honest heart of my deare freinde.

It is tyme to conclude, but I knowe not how to leave you, yet since I must, I will putt my beloved into his arms, who loves him best, and is a faithfull keeper of all that is Committed to him. Now thou the hope of Israell, and the sure helpe of all that come to thee, knitt the heartes of thy servantes to thy selfe, in faith and puritye: Drawe us with the sweetnesse of thine odours, that we may runne after thee, allure us, and speak kindly to thy servantes, that thou maist possesse us as thine owne, in the kindnesse of youthe and the love of mariage: sealle us up by that holy spirit of promise, that we may not feare to trust in thee: Carrye us into thy Garden, that we may eate and be filled with those pleasures, which the world knows not: let us heare that sweet voyce of thine, my love my dove, my undefiled: spread thy skirt over us and cover our deformitye, make us sicke with thy love: let us sleep in thine armes, and awake in thy kingdome: the soules of thy servantes, thus united to thee, make as one in the bonde of brotherly Affection.

PHILIPPE, DUC D'ORLÉANS
1640 – 1701

Philippe was the brother of Louis XIV ('le Roi-Soleil'). As a child he was dressed as a girl by order of a Cardinal, who wished to make him appear effeminate for fear he should become a rival to his brother. As an adult Philippe was described as 'a little pot-bellied man, looking as if mounted on stilts, so high were his heels; always decked out like a woman; covered all over with rings, bracelets and jewels; with a long wig all fluffy in front, black and powdered; with ribbons wherever he could bestow them and full of all sorts of perfumes.' However, Philippe was a good soldier, and performed with distinction in the war. He was married twice; his first wife was the seventeen-year-old Princess Henrietta Maria, daughter of Charles I of England, whom he married in 1661.

Here, Henrietta Maria writes to Anne de Gonzago with some general domestic anxieties, particularly concerning her husband's relationship with one Chevalier de Lorraine...

Saint Cloud, 29 June 1670

It is only right that I should give you an account of a voyage which your skill rendered acceptable in the only quarter where it might have failed. I will admit that on my return I was almost persuaded that I should find everybody contented. But I found matters worse than ever. You know – for you told me yourself on behalf of Monsieur – that he wished three things of me. Firstly, that he should share the confidential relations existing between the King my brother and myself; then, that I should arrange he should receive his son's income; lastly, that I should help the Chevalier de Lorraine. The King my brother – on the understanding that Monsieur would cease to behave in so bizarre a fashion as he has done over this journey – was good enough to agree to the first. Moreover he offered to receive the Chevalier de Lorraine in his Kingdom until things are quieter here. With regard to the pension, I have every hope of obtaining it, provided I can give an assurance that Monsieur will cease to play a comedy which has been performed too long in front of the public.

37

But you can quite understand that I am hardly able to ask for these things after Monsieur has done all he can to prevent me obtaining them. I must be assured of some domestic peace, and that he will not consider me responsible for everything that takes place in Europe. I have spoken to him about this, hardly doubting that it would be well received. But as there is no immediate probability of the Chevalier's return, Monsieur has said that everything else is useless, and that I need not expect his good graces until I allow him to have the Chevalier back again. I confess I am extremely surprised at this proceeding, which is very different from what I expected. Monsieur wishes to enjoy the friendship of the King my brother. When I offer it to him he receives it as if he conferred an honour on the King. He rejects the idea of allowing the Chevalier to spend a time in England, as if such matters can be arranged in a quarter of an hour. The pension he treats as a trifle. If he thought over the business he could not take up such an attitude. I can only suppose he prefers to remain on bad terms with me. The King has been good enough to declare to him on his oath that I have had nothing to do with the exile of the Chevalier, and that his return in no way depends upon me. Although the King has never told a lie, Monsieur refuses to believe him, and I shall be in a very unhappy position if I cannot arrange the business before it is too late.

There, my dear cousin, you have the state of my affairs. Monsieur has asked three things of me. I have been able to procure two and a half. He is angry because I cannot manage the whole, paying no attention to the offer of friendship from the King my brother, or to his own interests. Personally, I have done more than I expected. But, if I am unhappy enough to continue experiencing Monsieur's temper in all which concerns me, I declare, my dear cousin, I will give everything up…

It is easy to end the affair by keeping silent, a maxim Monsieur follows when I ask him for an explanation. As for the return of the Chevalier, if my credit were as strong as Monsieur imagines – I have already said it to you – nothing will ever make me give way to blows or force…

If he wishes me to act I will do it with joy. My only desire is to be on good terms with him. Otherwise I must bear his wicked treatment, against which I will never defend myself. I will give him no occasion to blame my conduct. His hatred is unreasonable, and I do not deserve it. I console myself with the hope that I shall receive more favourable consideration. You are able to do more than anyone, and I am convinced that Monsieur's interest and mine are equally dear to you. I trust that you will work to forward them.

On June 30th, 1670, the day after she had written the above letter, apparently in perfect health, Henrietta Maria died. Many thought that she had been poisoned by her husband's favourite, the Chevalier de Lorraine, and that the deadly medium had been added to her glass of chicory water. No proof was offered, and no charges were brought.

The following year, Philippe fell, by a Duke's standards, on hard times. He married again, this time to Elizabeth Charlotte of the Palatinate. She came with a large, and rescuing, dowry. She wrote copious and ingenuous letters to her family and friends, concerning her unusual husband...

Never were two brothers more totally different in their appearance. The king was tall, with light hair; his mien was good and his deportment manly. Monsieur, without looking vulgar, was very small. His hair and eyebrows were quite black; his eyes were dark, his face long and narrow, his nose large, his mouth small, and his teeth very bad. He was fond of cards, of holding drawing-rooms, of eating, dancing, and dress; in short, of all the things women like.

The King loved the chase, music and the theatre; my husband rather affected large assemblages and masquerades. His brother was a man of great gallantry, and I do not believe my husband was ever in love in his life. He danced well, but in a feminine manner; he could not dance like a man, because his shoes were too high-heeled. Except when with the army he would never mount a horse; the soldiers used to say he was more afraid of being sunburnt and the blackness of the powder, than of the musket-balls, and it was quite true.

Once, at a ball, Philippe disappeared to private rooms. He shortly reappeared, masked and dressed in skirts and a bodice. He danced a jaunty minuet with the Chevalier de Lorraine, then was escorted to a seat amidst the ladies. He took off his mask and sat 'playing the coquette', amusing his companions by sticking decorative patches, such as society women wore to cover blemishes, on his chin and cheeks.

Elizabeth Charlotte's enjoyable letters on the subject of Philippe were nothing if not frank ('he himself put the rouge upon my cheeks...'):

All my life since my youth I have found myself so ugly that I have never been tempted to adorn myself much. Jewels and fine toilets only attract attention to the people who wear them. It is well that I was in that humour, because Monsieur, who loved adornment exceedingly, would have had a thousand quarrels with me to decide who should wear the finest diamonds. Never have I adorned myself but that he ordained my toilet entirely. He himself put the rouge upon my cheeks.

In the light of Elizabeth Charlotte's views on her own lack of beauty, it is interesting to record that, when he first saw his future bride, the pot-bellied Philippe exclaimed: 'Oh! Comment pourrai-je coucher avec elle!' ('Oh! How shall I ever manage to go to bed with her!')

When his Grace slept in my bed, I had to lie on the edge, so that sometimes I fell out of the bed in my sleep. For his Grace could not endure to have me touch him, and if in my sleep I chanced to move my foot and do so, he would wake and scold me for half an hour. So I was heartily glad when his Grace made up his mind of his own accord to sleep in his own room and let me lie quiet without having to fear being scolded or falling out of bed.

To another friend she wrote:

Our heroes take as their models Hercules, Theseus, Alexander and Caesar, who all had their male favourites. Those who give themselves up to this vice, which believing in Holy Scripture, imagine that it was only a SIN when there were few people in the world, and that now the earth is populated it may be regarded as a divertissement.

Among the common people, indeed, accusations of this kind are so far as possible, avoided; but among persons of quality, it is publicly spoken of; it is considered a fine saying that since Sodom and Gomorrah, the Lord has punished no one for such offences.

Madame and Monsieur had three children: the Duc de Valois, who died aged three, the Duc de Chartres (the future Regent) and Elizabeth Charlotte, named after her mother. Monsieur had many new favourites (including the Duc de Gramont, Chevalier de Tilladet, Manicamp and the Marquis de Biran), but the gay côterie is believed to have dispersed after Monsieur had his bottom spanked in front of the King.

It seems that Monsieur was as profligate with his wife's money as he had been with his own before the marriage. He certainly was not spending it on his family...

1696

If it was only that Monsieur lost his money in gambling it would not be so bad; but that he gives it away by the hundreds of thousands of francs and then tries to economise it on his children and me is not pleasant at all.

They find that three young fellows alone received a hundred thousand thalers each year. There is no use expostulating with him, he says openly that he is growing old and has no time to lose. By hook or by crook he means to be merry to the end. Those who outlive him, he says, must shift for themselves, that he loves himself more than wife or children.

FRANCISCO CORREA NETTO
writing in 1664

Netto was the Sacristan at the Cathedral of Silves in Portugal. This passionate medley of letters, to guitarist and luthier Manuel Viegas, might be the earliest known sexually explicit gay love-letters in Europe. Unfortunately, even if the sex was shared, the passion seems to have been one-sided...

Senhor Manuel Viegas:

If men sleep with me, it is not to find a pussy. They place the cock between my legs, and there they have their way. I do not achieve it. If your Grace *[Vossa Merce]* would wish the same, dispose of me, I am at your service, to whom I swear unto death, to offer what is needed, and the losses are mine.

Francisco Correa Netto

Senhor Manuel Viegas:

Tender gift to me and longing to my senses, the tranquility of my thoughts about you is the proof of how much I desire and love you!

Now I shall not have peace nor hope of having you, because I see that not even with the best argument will my pledge serve you, heart wounded to death, heart never to be released from my affection for you.

My love and bounty: my feelings cannot rest an hour, either by day or night, without bringing to mind your companionship and your sweet words that are continually reflected in my memory.

Mirror of my sight and joy, if I have any right to you, bring peace to my heart and confirm the news I received this evening, that you were betrothed to a niece of Francisco Luiz last Monday. I would have said that by Easter you would be betrothed to me. You implied that often, and you gave your word on it. But do as you please: in spite of this I shall not stop doing what I can to be at your service. And remembering your arms and the kiss you gave me, that is what torments me most! And you know this subject well, in that heart of your loins, it was that which desired me, with its craving to fly up. There was no Lent for that heart in your loins, when I touched it with my fingers, and instantly it sprang up! And you, so evil, who did not want to do what comes so naturally!

Goodbye my darling, my happiness, my true love!

My idea is that, even though you may be married, you do not have to break your promise to be betrothed to your devoted Francisquinha. It seems to me you told Manoel da Costa that if I complied with your whims, even then you would come to me, because you do not care, and it was all sham.

Here is paper to answer: Now you have no excuse not to write for lack of paper.

Francisco Correa Netto

Manuel Viegas:

Our Lord allow you to live as many happy years as you desire!

I was not so black–hearted that you should say publicly that I should not go to your house. If you wished to say that, you should write or tell me privately. However, not even for this affront I become your enemy; and if you need something, advise me in writing.

I sent your clothes to be washed. Go to the house of Matias Araujo to order some shoes. And I will give you everything I have promised. And for the fiancée, thirty *alqueires* of wheat. As for my letters, tear them up, as I will destroy yours. Make me a guitar *[viola]* by your own hand, for which I will pay you. Heaven guard you all the years you desire, friend.

Francisco Correa Netto

False Traitor!

False deluded love: with what words can I express this sentiment? After Your Grace *(Vosa Merce)* left, news came to me that Your Grace intended to possess Maria Nunes, who does not conceal this from anyone, not even from me, saying that Your Grace gave some beads and pin money, saying that you desired her much. And en route to the shoemaker's to repair some shoes we talked about biscuits, and she said that Your Grace gave her some, and she said there were none so perfect. So it seems that Your Grace has a great love for her, because she says that you come from your lovers, bringing her their gifts.

43

My destiny is wretched, I was confident until this, thinking that I possessed Your Grace. Better that I were put to death a thousand times than to live with something that I remember that I did to some person some time ago. But after all, if she goes around telling everyone that she saw what you gave me on my finger, my heart will burst within my chest, and I had to excuse this by saying that I had purchased the ring from Your Grace. *Vossa Merce* has left my heart besieged, with my sentiments manifest in my tears; and when I see the person I desire, I am sad and jealous, and so Your Grace grows happier. As the proverb says, 'One remembers where the honey was' [*'O mel faz por onde o lembrem'*], and this is how I must be with your Grace, inasmuch as Your Grace pays so little attention. Your Grace has so many, and one will be the worse for it, and I am that one, because I had such love for Your Grace, that just seeing you made me so happy that I could not eat. It is certain that 'whoever loves more strongly deserves least' [*quem mais ama, menos merece*]. I will leave my heart afar, and I will look at the ground whenever I pass Your Grace.

Heaven protect Your Grace for the sake of your two lovers!

Francisco Correa Netto

False and Flatterer:

If I could mock, scoffing at someone in love! But in the end, *quem mais ama menos merece*. For me there were only tears, tears caused by you and by so many skirts. Now she has what I desired. So often I have sent you word not to pay attention to me, but why do you dine with your women friends rather than with me, and then why do you send me notes that are lies? Those women were jealous of me because I wore someone else's ring. They said I should return it to its owner. And here it is. I don't want anything of yours in my possession. Do the same with what you have of mine, and that will give me much pleasure. Do not ever speak to me or look at me again. I return the ring to encourage the hilarity of your lady friends.

Manuel Viegas finally betrayed his ardent lover by passing these desperate letters to a vicar of the church, who in turn passed them on to the Inquisition of Evora, denouncing Netto for sodomy. Happily, Netto was never brought to trial.

FREDERICK THE GREAT
(Frederick II of Prussia)
1712 – 1786

As a boy, Frederick pursued literature and music, to the consternation of his father, Frederick William I, who hardened the boy up with the toughest of regimes. Young Frederick planned to flee with his lover, Hans de Katte, at the age of eighteen. They were discovered and imprisoned. Frederick was forced to watch de Katte's execution – a beheading – and then undertake an arranged marriage. This was childless, and he continued to take male lovers. These included Baron Trenck, Count Kayserlinck and Barbarini. Attitudes at the Prussian court made life impossible for a gay man. To his nephew, he once wrote; 'I can assure you, from my own personal experience, that this Greek pleasure is not a pleasant one to cultivate.'

Frederick became a great conquering soldier and an enlightened and benevolent despot, perhaps influenced by the correspondence he began at the age of twenty-four with Voltaire (1694–1778)…

From Frederick, Prince Royal of Prussia

Berlin, 8th August, 1736

Sir,

Although I have not the satisfaction of knowing you personally, you are none the less known to me by your works. They are treasures of the mind, if the expression may be allowed, and compositions elaborated with so much taste, delicacy, and art, that their beauties appear new each time they are re-read. I feel I have discovered in them the character of their ingenious author, who does honour to our age and to the human mind. The great men of modern times will one day be obliged to you, and to you alone, if the dispute concerning the ancients and the moderns should again arise: because you will incline the balance to their side.

To the quality of an excellent poet you add an infinity of other knowledge which indeed has some affinity with poetry but has only been fitted to it by your pen. Never before has a poet made metaphysical thought rhythmic; you were the first for whom that honour was reserved. That taste for philosophy which you display in your writings encourages me to send you a translation I have had made of the accusation and justification of M. Wolff, the most celebrated philosopher of our days, who has been cruelly accused of irreligion and atheism because he carried light into the most shadowy recesses of metaphysics and because he treated this difficult subject in a manner as elevated as it was clear and precise. Such is the destiny of great men: their superior genius ever leaves them naked to the poisoned darts of calumny and envy.

I am now having translated a *Treatise on God, the Soul and the World*, which emanates from the pen of the same author. It shall be sent to you, Sir, as soon as it is finished, and I am sure you will be struck by the force of evidence in all its propositions, which follow each other geometrically and are connected together like the links of a chain.

The complacency and support you exhibit towards all who devote themselves to the arts and sciences make me hope that you will not exclude me from the number of those whom you find worthy of your instruction. I mean your correspondence; which cannot but be profitable to every thinking being. Without aspersing the deserts of others, I dare to assert that the whole world cannot show a person to whom you could not act as a master. Without overwhelming you with an incense unworthy to be offered you, I must yet say that I find numberless beauties in your works. Your *Henriade* charms me and triumphs happily over the injudicious criticisms which have been made of it. The tragedy of César shows us sustained characters; its sentiments are all magnificent and grand; and we realise that Brutus is either a Roman or an Englishman. *Alzire* adds to the graces of novelty the happy contrast between the manners of savages and of Europeans. Through the character Gusman you show us that Christianity when misconceived and guided by false zeal renders men more barbarous and cruel than Paganism itself. If Corneille, the great Corneille, who attracted the admiration of his age, should come to life again in our days, he would see with astonishment and perhaps with envy that the goddess of Tragedy lavishes prodigally upon you those favours of which she was so sparing to him. What may we not expect from the author of so many masterpieces! What fresh wonders may not issue from the pen, which lately designed so wittily and elegantly the Temple of Taste!

This it is which makes me desire so ardently to possess all your works. I beg you to send them to me, sir, and to communicate them unreservedly. If among your manuscripts there should be any which, with necessary prudence, you think fit to hide from the public eye, I promise you to keep it secret and to content myself with applauding it in private. I know unfortunately that the faith of princes is little to be trusted in our days; yet I hope you will not allow yourself to be moved by general prejudices and that you will make an exception to the rule in my favour.

In possessing your works I should think myself richer than in possessing all the transitory and contemptible gifts of fortune which are acquired and lost by a like chance. The first can be made our own – I mean your works – by the aid of memory, and remain ours as long as it does. Knowing the slight extent of my own memory I reflect long before choosing those things I consider worthy of being placed in it.

If poetry were in the same condition as it was formerly, that is if poets could do nothing but hum over tedious idylls, eclogues cast in one mould and insipid stanzas, or if they could do nothing but raise their lyres to the tone of elegy, I should renounce it for ever; but you ennoble this art, you show us new paths and roads unknown to the Lefrancs and the Rousseaus.

Your poems possess qualities which render them respectable and worthy of the admiration and study of good men. They are a course of morality whereby we learn to think and to act. Virtue is painted there in its fairest colours. The idea of true glory is there defined; and you insinuate the taste of knowledge in a manner so fine and so delicate that he who has read your works breathes the ambition of following in your steps. How often have I said to myself: 'Wretched man! abandon this burden whose weight exceeds your strength; Voltaire cannot be imitated except by Voltaire himself.'

At such moments I have realised that the advantages of birth and that vapour of grandeur with which vanity soothes us is of little service or, to speak truly, of none.

These distinctions are foreign to ourselves and but embellish outwardly. How much more preferable are the talents of the mind! How much is due to men whom nature has distinguished by the mere fact that she has created them! She takes pleasure in creating some whom she endows with every capacity needed for the progress of the arts and sciences; 'tis for princes to reward their vigils. Ah! may glory only make use of me to crown your successes! I should fear nothing except that this country is so infertile in laurels that it does not furnish as many as your works deserve.

If I am not so favoured by my destiny as to take you into my service, at least I may hope one day to see you, whom I have admired so long and from so far, and to assure you by word o' mouth that I am, with all the esteem and consideration due to those who, following the torch of truth, devote their labours to the public, Sir, your affectionate friend,

Fédéric, P.R. of Prussia

The young Prince Frederick may have been seeking a guru, but the older man of forty-two laid down the ground-rules for their relationship...

Paris, 26th August, 1736

Monseigneur,

I should indeed be insensitive were I not infinitely touched by the letter with which your Royal Highness has been graciously pleased to honour me. My self–love was but too flattered; but that love of the human race which has always existed in my heart and which I dare to say determines my character, gave me a pleasure a thousand times purer when I saw that the world holds a prince who thinks like a man, a philosophical prince who will make men happy.

Suffer me to tell you that there is no man on the earth who should not return thanks for the care you take in cultivating by sane philosophy a soul born to command. Be certain there have been no truly good kings except those who began like you, by educating themselves, by learning to know men, by loving the truth, by detesting persecution and superstition. Any prince who thinks in this way can bring back the golden age to his dominions. Why do so few kings seek out this advantage? You perceive the reason, Monseigneur; it is because almost all of them think more of royalty than of humanity: you do precisely the opposite. If the tumult of affairs and the malignancy of men do not in time alter so divine a character, you will be adored by your people and admired by the whole world. Philosophers worthy of that name will fly to your dominions; and, as celebrated artists crowd to that country where their art is most favoured, men who think will press forward to surround your throne.

The illustrious Queen Christina left her kingdom to seek the arts; reign, Monseigneur, and let the arts come to seek you.

May you never be disgusted from the sciences by the quarrels of learned men! From those circumstances which you were graciously pleased to inform me of, Monseigneur, you see that most of them are men like courtiers themselves. They are sometimes as greedy, as intriguing, as treacherous, as cruel; and the only difference between the pests of the court and the pests of the school is that the latter are the more ridiculous.

It is very sad for humanity that those who term themselves the messengers of Heaven's command, the interpreters of the Divinity, in a word theologians, are sometimes the most dangerous of all; that some of them are as pernicious to society as they are obscure in their ideas and that their souls are inflated with bitterness and pride in proportion as they are empty of truths. For the sake of a sophism they would trouble the earth and would persuade all kings to avenge with fire and steel the honour of an argument *in ferio* or *in barbara*.

Every thinking being not of their opinion is an atheist; and every king who does not favour them will be damned. You know, Monseigneur, that the best one can do is to leave to themselves these pretended teachers and real enemies of the human race. Their words, when unheeded, are lost in the air like wind; but if the weight of authority is lent them, this wind acquires a force which sometimes overthrows the throne itself.

I see, Monseigneur, with the joy of a heart filled with love of the public weal, the immense distance you set between men who seek the truth in peace and those who would make war for words they do not understand. I see that Newton, Leibnitz, Bayle, Locke, those elevated minds, so enlightened, so gentle, have nourished your spirit and that you reject other pretended nourishment which you find poisoned or without substance.

I cannot sufficiently thank your Royal Highness for your kindness in sending me the little book about M. Wolff. I look upon his metaphysical ideas as things which do honour to the human mind. They are flashes in the midst of a dark night; and that, I think, is all we can hope of metaphysics. It seems improbable that the first principles of things will ever be thoroughly known. The mice living in a few little holes of an immense building do not know if the building is eternal, who is the architect, or why the architect built it. They try to preserve their lives, to people their holes, and to escape the destructive animals which pursue them. We are the mice; and the divine architect who built this universe has not yet, so far as I know, told His secret to any of us. If any man can pretend to have guessed accurately, it is M. Wolff. He may be combatted, but he must be esteemed; his philosophy is far from being pernicious; is there anything more beautiful and more true than to say, as he does, that men should be just even if they were so unfortunate as to be atheists?

The protection you appear to give, Monseigneur, to this learned man, is a proof of the accuracy of your mind and of the humanity of your sentiments.

You have the kindness, Monseigneur, to promise that you will send me the *Treatise on God, the Soul and the World*. What a present, Monseigneur, and what an interchange! The heir of a monarchy deigns to send instruction from the heart of his palace to a solitary! Be graciously pleased to send me this present, Monseigneur; my extreme love of truth is the one thing which makes me worthy of it. Most princes fear to listen to the truth, but you will teach it.

As to the verses you speak of – you think as wisely of this art as in everything else. Verses which do not teach men new and moving truths do not deserve to be read. You perceive that there is nothing more contemptible than for a man to spend his life in rhyming worn–out commonplaces which do not deserve the name of thoughts. If there is anything viler it is to be nothing but a satirical poet and to write only to decry others. Such poets are to Parnassus what those doctors, who know nothing but words and intrigue against those who write things, are to the schools.

If *La Henriade* did not displease your Royal Highness I must thank that love of truth, that horror which my poem inspires for the factious, for persecutors, for the superstitious, for tyrants and for rebels. 'Tis the work of an honest man; and should find grace in the eyes of a philosophic prince.

You command me to send you my other work; I shall obey you, Monseigneur; you shall be my judge, you shall stand to me in lieu of the public. I will submit to you what I have attempted in philosophy; your instruction shall be my reward: 'tis a prize which few sovereigns can give. I am certain of your secrecy; your virture must be equal to your knowledge.

I should consider it a most valuable privilege to wait upon your Royal Highness. We go to Rome to see churches, pictures, ruins and bas–reliefs. A prince like yourself is far more deserving of a journey; 'tis a more marvellous rarity. But friendship, which holds me in my retreat, does not permit me to leave it. Doubtless you think like Julian, that calumniated great man, who said that friends should always be preferred to kings.

In whatever corner of the world I end my life, be certain, Monseigneur, that I shall constantly wish you well, and in doing so wish the happiness of a nation. My heart will be among your subjects; your fame will ever be dear to me. I shall wish that you may always be like yourself and that other kings may be like you. I am with deep respect your Royal Highness's most humble, etc.

Voltaire

THOMAS GRAY
1716 – 1771

Thomas Gray wrote many beautiful poems, including the evocative 'Elegy Written in a Country Churchyard', and for his friend Horace Walpole 'Ode on the Death of a Favourite Cat'. He was close to his mother, who was treated harshly by his father. He went to Eton in 1725, where he met Horace Walpole and Richard West.

West graduated to Christchurch, Oxford, from where he corresponded with Thomas Gray:

From Mr West to Mr Gray

You use me very cruelly: you have sent me but one letter since I have been at Oxford, and that too agreeable not to make me sensible how great my loss is not having more. Next to seeing you is the pleasure of seeing your hand-writing; next to hearing you is the pleasure of hearing from you. – Really and sincerely I wonder at you, that you thought it not worth while to answer my last letter. I hope this will have better success in behalf on your quondom school-fellow; in behalf of one who has walked hand in hand with you, like the two children in the wood,

> Through many a flowery path and shelly grot,
> Where learning lulled us in her private maze.

The very thought, you see, tips my pen with poetry, and brings Eton to my view. Consider me very seriously here in a strange country, inhabited by things that call themselves doctors and masters of arts; a country flowing with syllogisms and ale, where Horace and Virgil are equally unknown; consider me, I say, in this melancholy light, and then think if something be not due to

Yours

Christ Church, Nov. 14, 1735

To Mr West

Permit me again to write to you, though I have so long neglected my duty and forgive my brevity, when I tell you, it is occasioned wholly by the hurry I am in to get to a place where I expect to meet no other pleasure than the sight of you; for I am preparing for London in a few days at furthest. I do not wonder in the least at your frequent blaming my indolence – it aught rather to be called ingratitude, and I am obliged to your goodness for softening so harsh an appellation. When we meet, it will however be my greatest pleasure to know what you do, what you read, and how you spend your time etc etc, and to tell you what I do not read, and how I do not, etc for almost all the employment of my hours may be best explained by negatives; take my word and experience upon it, doing nothing is a most amusing business; and yet neither something nor nothing gives me any pleasure. When you have seen one of my days, you have seen a whole year of my life; they go round and round like the blind horse in the mill, only he has the satisfaction of fancying he makes a progress, and gets some ground; my eyes are open enough to see the same dull prospect, and to know that having made four-and-twenty steps more, I shall be just where I was...

However, as the most undeserving people in the world must sure have the vanity to wish somebody had a regard for them, so I need not wonder at my own, in being pleased that you care about me. You need not doubt, therefore, of having a first row in the front box of my little heart, and I believe you are not in danger of being crowded there; it is asking you to an old play, indeed, but you will be candid enough to excuse the whole piece for the sake of a few tolerable lines.
Cambridge, May 8, 1736

West died tragically at twenty-six. Gray commemorated the day with 'A Sonnet On the Death of Richard West', and mourned his great friend for many years, pouring his sadness into his poems. However, in 1769, he met Charles Victor de Bonstetten, a popular and handsome young Swiss nobleman, with whom he (and many others) fell quite in love ('I never saw such a boy; our breed is not made on this model')...

Cambridge, April 12, 1770

Never did I feel, my dear Bonstetten, to what a tedious length the few short moments of our life may be extended by impatience and expectation, till you had left me; nor never knew before with so strong a conviction how much this frail body sympathizes with the inquietude of mind. I am grown old in the compass of less than three weeks. The strength and spirits that now enable me to write to you, are only owing to your last letter – a temporary gleam of sunshine. Heaven knows when it may shine again! I did not conceive till now, I own, what it was to lose you, nor felt the solitude and insipidity of my own condition before I possessed the happiness of your friendship. I must cite another Greek writer to you, because it is much to my purpose: he is describing the character of a genius truly inclined to philosophy. 'It includes', he says, 'qualifications rarely united in one single mind, quickness of apprehension and a retentive memory, vivacity and application, gentleness and magnanimity; to these he adds an invincible love of truth, and consequently of probity and justice. 'Such a soul', continues he, 'will be little inclined to sensual pleasures, and consequently temperate; a stranger to illiberality and avarice; being accustomed to the most extensive views of things, and sublimest contemplations, it will contract an habitual greatness, will look down with a kind of disregard on human life and on death, consequently, will possess the truest fortitude'. 'Such', says he, 'is the mind borne to govern the rest of mankind: But these very endowments so necessary to the soul – a soul formed for philosophy, are often its ruin, especially when joined to the external advantages of wealth, nobility, strength and beauty; that is, if it light on bad soil, and want its proper nurture, which nothing but an excellent education can bestow. In this case he is depraved by the public example, the assemblies of people, the courts of justice, the theatres, that inspire it with false opinions, terrify it with false infamy, or elevate it with false applause; and remember, that extraordinary views and extraordinary virtues are equally the produce of a vigorous mind; little souls are alike incapable of the one and the other.

If you have ever met with the portrait sketched out by Plato, you will know it again: for my part, to my sorrow I have had that happiness; I see the principal features, and I forsee the dangers with a trembling anxiety. But enough of this; I return to your letter. It proves at least, that in the midst of your new gaieties I still hold some place in your memory, and what pleases me above all, it has an air of undissembled sincerity. Go on, my best and amiable friend, to show me your heart simply and without the shadow of disguise, and leave me to weep over it, as I now do, no matter whether from joy or sorrow.

May 9 1770

I am returned, my dear Bonstetten, from the little journey I made into Suffolk, without answering the end proposed. The thought that you might have been with me there has embittered all my hours: your letter has made me happy, as happy as so gloomy so solitary a being as I am is capable of being made. I know, and have too often felt the disadvantages I lay myself under, how much I hurt the little interest I have in you, but this air of sadness so contrary to your nature and present enjoyments: but sure you will forgive though you cannot sympathize with me. It is impossible for me to dissemble with you; such as I am I expose my heart to your view, nor wish to conceal a single thought from your penetrating eyes.

All that you say to me especially on the subject of Switzerland, is infinitely acceptable. It feels too pleasing ever to be fulfilled, and as often as I read over your truly kind letter, written long since from London, I stop at these words:

'La mort qui peut glacer nos bras avant qu'ils soient entrelacés.' ['Death, who can freeze our arms before they are intertwined.']

HORACE WALPOLE
1717 – 1797

Walpole was educated at Eton, where, with his friends Thomas Gray (q.v.), Richard West (q.v.) and Thomas Ashton he formed 'The Quadrupal Alliance'. At King's College, Cambridge, his circle included Henry Seymour Conway and George Montagu, both of whom became lifetime friends. Walpole went into politics, eventually inheriting the Earldom of Orford. In 1747 he bought a small house in Twickenham, 'Strawberry Hill', where he installed a printing press in 1755. Some of his friend Gray's work was printed on this press.

Walpole wrote Historic Doubts on the Life and Reign of King Richard the Third, Memoirs of the Last Ten Years of the Reign of George II *and* Memoirs of the Reign of King George III, *and the first Gothic novel* The Castle of Otranto. *Above all he is celebrated for his prolific and excellent correspondence, published posthumously in at least sixteen volumes.*

Horace Walpole never married, and the critic Leigh Hunt wrote of Walpole's relationship with his tenant, the actress Kitty Clive, that his 'effeminacy she helped to keep on the alert. It always seems to us as if she had been the man of the two and he the woman.'

Here, on a continental tour with Thomas Gray, he writes to Richard West:

To Richard West

Rheims, July 20, 1739

Gray says, Indeed you ought to write to West. – Lord, child, so I would, if I knew what to write about. If I were in London and he at Rheims, I would send him volumes about peace and war, Spaniards, camps, and conventions; but d'ye think he cares sixpence to know who is gone to Compiègne, and when they come back, or who won and lost four livres at quadrille last night at Mr. Cockbert's? – No, but you may tell him what you have heard of Compiègne; that they have balls twice a week after the play, and that the Count d'Eu gave the king a most flaring entertainment in the camp, where the Polygone was represented in flowering shrubs. Dear West, these are the things I must tell you; I don't know how to make 'em look significant, unless you be a Rhemois for a little moment. I wonder you can stay out of the city so long, when we are going to have all manner of diversions. The

56

comedians return hither from Compiègne in eight days, for example; and in a very little of time one attends the regiment of the king, three battalions and an hundred of officers; all men of a certain fashion, very amiable, and who know their world. Our women grow more gay, more lively, from day to day, in expecting them; Mademoiselle la Reine is brewing a wash of a finer dye, and brushing up her eyes for their arrival. La Baronne already counts upon fifteen of them: and Madame Lelu, finding her linen robe conceals too many beauties, has bespoke one of gauze.

I won't plague you any longer with people you don't know, I mean French ones; for you must absolutely hear of an Englishman that lately appeared at Rheims. About two days ago, about four o'clock in the afternoon, and about an hour after dinner, – from all which you may conclude we dine at two o'clock, – as we were picking our teeth round a littered table and in a crumby room, Gray in an undress, Mr. Conway in a morning grey coat, and I in a trim white night–gown and slippers, very much out of order, with a very little cold, a message discomposed us all of a sudden, with a service to Mr. Walpole from Mr. More, and that, if he pleased, he would wait on him. We scuttle upstairs in great confusion, but with no other damage than the flinging down two or three glasses and the dropping a slipper by the way. Having ordered the room to be cleaned out, and sent a very civil response to Mr. More, we began to consider who Mr. More should be. Is it Mr. More of Paris? No. Oh, 'tis Mr. More, my Lady Teynham's husband? No, it can't be he. A Mr. More, then, that lives in the Halifax family? No. in short, after thinking of ten thousand more Mr. Mores, we concluded it could never be a one of 'em. By this time Mr. More arrives; but such a Mr. More! a young gentleman out of the wilds of Ireland, who has never been in England, but has got all the ordinary language of that kingdom; has been two years at Paris, where he dined at an ordinary with the refugee Irish, and learnt fortifications, which he does not understand at all, and which yet is the only thing he knows. In short, he is a young swain of very uncouth phrase, inarticulate speech, and no ideas. This hopeful child is riding post into Lorrain, or anywhere else, he is not certain; for if there is a war he shall go home again: for we must give the Spaniards another drubbing, you know; and if the Dutch do but join us, we shall blow up all the ports in Europe; for our ships are our bastions, and our ravelins, and our hornworks; and there's a devilish wide ditch for 'em to pass, which they can't fill up with things. – Here Mr. Conway helped him to fascines. By this time I imagine you have laughed at him as much, and were as tired of him as we were: but he's gone. This is the day that Gray and I intended for the first of a southern circuit; but as Mr. Selwyn and George Montagu design us a visit here, we have put off our journey for some weeks. When we get a little farther, I hope our memoires will brighten: at present they are but dull, dull as

Your humble servant ever,
H.W.

P.S. I thank you ten thousand times for your last letter: when I have as much wit and as much poetry in me, I'll send you as good an one. Good night, child!

Walpole writes to his good friend George Montagu, concerning life at 'Strawberry Hill':

To George Montagu

Strawberry Hill, Oct. 14, 1756

I shall certainly not bid for the chariot for you; do you estimate an old dowager's new machine but at ten pounds? You could scarce have valued herself at less! it is appraised here at fifty. There are no family pictures but such as you might buy at any perpetual sale, that is, there are three portraits without names. If you had offered ten pounds for a set of Pelhams, perhaps I should not have thought you had under-prized them.

You bid me give you some account of myself; I can in very few words: I am quite alone; in the morning I view a new pond I am making for gold-fish, and stick in a few shrubs or trees, wherever I can find a space, which is very rare: in the evening I scribble a little; all this mixed with reading, that is, I can't say I read much, but I pick up a good deal of reading. The only thing I have done that can compose a paragraph, and which I think you are Whig enough to forgive me, is, that on each side of my bed I have hung the *Magna Charta*, and the Warrant for King Charles's execution, on which I have written Major Charta, as I believe, without the latter, the former by this time would be of very little importance. You will ask where Mr. Bentley is; confined with five sick infantas, who live in spite of the epidemic distemper, and as if they were infantas, and in bed himself with a fever and the same sore throat, though he sends me word he mends.

The King of Prussia has sent us over a victory; which is very kind, as we are not likely to get any of our own – not even by the secret expedition, which you apprehend, and which I believe still less than I did the invasion. – Perhaps indeed there may be another port on the coast of France which we hope to discover, as we did one in the last war. By degrees, and somehow or other, I believe, we shall be fully acquainted with France. I saw the German letter you mention, think it very mischievous, and very well written for the purpose.

You talk of being better than you have been for many months; pray, which months were they, and what was the matter with you? Don't send me your fancies; I shall neither pity nor comfort you. You are perfectly well, and always was ever since I knew you, which is now – I won't say how long, but within this century. Thank God you have good health, and don't call it names. John and I are just going to Garrick's with a grove of cypresses in our hands, like the Kentish men at the Conquest. He has built a temple to his master Shakespear, and I am going to adorn the outside, since his modesty would not let me decorate it within, as I proposed, with these mottoes:

Quod spiro et placco, si placco, tuum est.

That I spirit have and nature,
That sense breathes in ev'ry feature,
That I please, if please I do,
Shakespear, all I owe to you.

Adieu!
Yours ever,
H.W.

JOHANN JOACHIM WINCKELMANN
1717 – 1768

The son of a poor Brandenburg cobbler, Winckelmann became a great scholar, the inspiration of modern archaeology and the first published art critic. Goethe said he was a 'natural pagan'. Winckelmann felt, as Walter Pater said, 'The Protestant principle in Art had cut off Germany from the supreme tradition of beauty.' In 1764 he wrote his masterpiece: Geschichte der Kunst des Alterthums *('History of Ancient Art'). Despite two recorded affairs in Rome (with Franz Stander and Niccolo Castellani), Winckelmann's real love was for a certain Friedrich von Berg. To von Berg, Winckelmann once wrote; 'As a solicitous mother inconsolably mourns her beloved child, so my sweet friend, I deplore our separation with all my heart... My beloved and very beautiful friend, all the names I could call you are not tender enough and do not express the fullness of my love... I love you more than any living thing, and neither time nor chance nor age can ever lessen this love.'*

Here he writes to Count Bruhl of Saxony on the wonders of the new discoveries at Herculaneum, near Pompeii:

Sir,

As I had the honour to accompany you in the tour you made from Rome to Naples, during the carnival of the year 1762, I thought it would not be amiss to commit to writing some of the observations on the curiosities we saw... I promised to speak of the works of art, those introduced by opulence and luxury.

Among the silver bodkins used to roll up the hair, and keep it to the back of the head, there are four of uncommon size and workmanship; for this was one of the ornaments which most deserved the attention of the sex. The eunuchs of the priests of Cybele made use of bodkins with heads for the same purpose. The largest of those above mentioned in a Corinthian capital, instead of a round knob with a Venus on it, holding her hair with both hands; and near her, a Cupid presenting her with a circular glass. It was customary with the Roman ladies to consecrate looking-glasses to the statues of their Divinities of their feast-days. The silver bodkins, still in use among country women about Naples, are of the same length...

In the same apartment are to be seen gold, and some brazen bracelets, all in the form of a serpent, and of the smallest kind, being such as used to be worn on the wrists... The gold ear-rings resemble the head of an acorn, adorned with little projecting buckles, their openings turned towards the ear. The women in the neighbourhood of Naples still wear them of the same form.

The Pateræ, which I reckon, as I have already observed, in the class of household utensils, are of an artificial white metal, which, at first sight, one would be apt to take for silver, and has this quality in common with silver, that it breeds a kind of verdigrease.

Who knows, – but it may be one of the famous metals of Corinth, or Syracuse? What deserves our attention most, in the utensils of the ancients, particularly their vessels, is the elegant form of them; a circumstance in which our modern artists must yield to the ancients. All those beautiful forms are founded on the principle of good taste, and may be compared with those of a handsome young man, whose attitudes abound with natural graces. It may be said that this graceful-ness extends even to the handles and ears of their vessels. Would our artists but endeavour to imitate them, their works would soon put on another taste. They would put on such a face as, by removing us from art, would bring us back to nature, by which art might afterwards be improved. The chief beauty of these vessels consists of the softness and smoothness of their contours, little differing from those which, in the bodies of well-made youths, have a certain elegance not to be met with in equal perfection in those of grown up persons. Our eyes do not love to be bounded by complete semi-circles, or stopped by salient points or angles. The secret sensation our eyes experience, when we look at pure and simple forms, is like that produced by the touching of a tender and delicate skin... It looks, I say, as if our own feelings and reflections should alone be sufficient to bring us back to the beautiful simplicity of the ancients.

If this letter should reach you, Sir, while on your travels, accept with it of my most ardent wishes that Providence may every where direct your steps, and bring you back in good health and rich in useful knowledge to our dear country...

I presume to hope that I shall ever preserve that share of your affections with which you have condescended to honour me.

Winckelmann's death was ugly. In 1768 he was in Vienna. There he was loaded with favours by the Empress, Queen Maria Theresa, who gave him three valuable gold medals. Returning to Rome via Trieste, he stayed at the Locanda Grande Hotel in that city, where he passed his time with Francesco Arcangeli, an ex-convict. The two men enjoyed the city, touring the great buildings and artefacts. After several days, Arcangeli stabbed and strangled the great scholar in the hotel room, in a second snuffing out one of the finest minds of his age. Arcangeli was eventually captured and executed. Curiously he had not stolen the gold medals.

LORD BYRON
1788 – 1824

George Noel Gordon Byron, English poet and satirist, inherited Newstead
Abbey and his title in 1798 from an uncle. At Harrow he developed passions
for two fellow students: Lord Clare and Lord Dorset. Byron was good at sport,
despite his club foot. At Cambridge University he began to write poetry, and
fell in love with seventeen-year-old choirboy John Eddleston. Eddleston died at
twenty-two and Byron must have missed him enormously. He had written: 'I
certainly love him more than any human being... During the whole of my
residence at Cambridge we met every day, Summer and Winter, without
passing one tiresome moment, and separated each hour with increasing
reluctance...'

In 1809 Byron undertook his famous 'Grand Tour' with his friend John
Cam Hobhouse. He wrote thrilling letters to his mother, regaling her with his
adventures, including his amazing swim across the Hellespont ('Sea of Helle')
in Greece:

To the Honourable Mrs. Byron

> Constantinople, May 18th, 1810

Dear Madam,

I arrived here in a English frigate from Smyrna a few days ago,
without any events worth mentioning, except landing to view the
plains of Troy, and afterwards, when we were at anchor in the
Dardanelles, 'swimming' from Sestos to Abydos, in imitation of
Monsieur Leander, whose story you no doubt know too well for me to
add anything on the subject, except that I crossed the Hellespont
without so good a motive for the undertaking. As I am just going to
visit the Captain Pacha, you will excuse the brevity of my letter. When
Mr. Adair takes leave, I am to see the Sultan and the mosques etc.

> Believe me,
> Yours ever,
> Byron

Lord Byron's Childe Harold, a poetical autobiography, was published by John Murray and made Byron's name.

Byron once said: 'I could love anything on earth that appeared to wish it'. Despite his feelings for his closest male friends, Byron was devoted to the eccentric Caroline Lamb, with whom he had an affair, following this with what are described as 'intimate relations' with his half-sister Augusta Leigh, finally marrying Isabella Millbanke in 1815. A year later, after the birth of their daughter Augusta, Isabella returned to her father; it was said that Byron's sexual demands on her were unusual and distasteful to her, though he claimed she had enjoyed them at the time.

Byron returned to Athens, where he had a passionate love affair with a French/Greek boy Nicolo Giraud ('the most beautiful being I ever beheld'). At one stage in their relationship it is recorded that Byron consulted an English doctor on his friend's behalf, concerning 'the relaxation of the sphincter ani'.

Byron was a prolific correspondent; his collected letters to family and friends fill many volumes...

Newstead Abbey, Sept. 3, 1811

My Dear Hodgson, – I will have nothing to do with your immortality; we are miserable enough in this life *[The religious discussion arose out of the opening stanzas of* Childe Harold, *Canto II, which Hodgson was helping to correct for the press]* without the absurdity of speculating upon another. If men are to live, why die at all? and if they die, why disturb the sweet and sound sleep that 'knows no waking'? 'Post Mortem nihil est, ipasque Mors nihil '...quæris quo jaceas post obitum loco? Quo *non* 'Nata jacent'. *[From Seneca's* Troades*]*.

As to revealed religion, Christ came to save men; but a good Pagan will go to heaven, and a bad Nazarene to hell; 'Agal' (I argue like the gravedigger) why are not all men Christians? or why are any? If mankind may be saved who never heard or dreamt, at Timbuctoo, Otaheite, Terra Incognita, etc., of Galilee and its Prophet, Christianity is of no avail: if they cannot be saved without, why are not all orthodox? It is a little hard to send a man preaching to Judea, and leave the rest of the world – Negers and what not – dark as their complexions, without a ray of light for so many years to lead them on high; and who will believe that God will damn men for not knowing what they were taught? I hope I am sincere; I was so at least on a bed of sickness in a far distant country, when I had neither friend, nor comforter, nor hope, to sustain me. I looked to death as a relief from pain, without a wish for an after-life, but a confidence that the God who punishes in this existence had left that last asylum for the weary.

I am no Platonist, I am nothing at all; but I would sooner be a Paulician, Manichean, Spionozist, Gentile, Pyrrhonian, Zoroastrian, than one of the seventy-two villainous sects who are tearing each other to pieces for the love of the Lord and hatred of each other. Talk of Galileeism? Show me the effects – are you better, wiser, kinder by your precepts. I will bring you ten Mussulmans shall shame you in all goodwill towards men, prayer to God and duty to their neighbours. And is there a Talapoin, or a Bronze, who is not superior to a fox-hunting curate? But I will say no more on this endless theme, let me live, well if possible, and die without pain. The rest is with God, who assuredly, had He *come* or *sent* would have made Himself manifest to nations, and intelligible to all.

I shall rejoice to see you.

Yours ever.

BN.

Byron, adopting the literary style and name of his own valet, Fletcher, writes to a friend, John Cam Hobhouse:

Venice, June 1818

Sir, – With great grief I inform you of the death of my late dear Master, my Lord, who died this morning at ten of the Clock of a rapid decline and slow fever, caused by anxiety, sea-bathing, women, and riding in the Sun against my advice.

He is a dreadful loss to everybody, mostly to me, who have lost a master and a place – also, I hope you, Sir, will give me a charakter.

I saved in his service as you know several hundred pounds. God knows how, for I don't nor my late master neither; and if my wage was not always paid to the day, still it was or is to be paid sometime and somehow. You Sir, who are his executioner won't see a poor Servant wronged of his little all.

My dear Master had several physicians and a Priest: he died a Papist, but is to be buried among the Jews in the Jewish burying ground; for my part I don't see why – he could not abide them when living nor any other people, hating whores who asked him for money.

He suffered his illness with great patience, except that when in extremity he twice damned his friends and said they were selfish rascals – you, Sir, particularly and Mr. Kinnaird, who had never answered his letters nor complied with his repeated requests. He also said he hoped that your new tragedy would be damned – God forgive him – I hope that my master won't be damned like the tragedy.

His nine whores are already provided for, and the other servants; but what is to become of me? I have got his Clothes and Carriages, and Cash, and everything, but the Consul quite against law has clapt his seal and taken an inventory and swears that *he* must account to my Lord's heirs – who they are, I don't know – but they ought to consider poor Servants and above all his Vally de Sham.

My Lord never grudged me perquisites – my wage was the least I got by him; and if I did keep the Countess (she is, or ought to be, a Countess, although she is upon the town) Marietta Monetta Piretta, after passing my word to you and my Lord that I would not never no more – still he was an indulgent master, and only said I was a damned fool, and swore and forgot it again. What could I do? she said as how she should die, or kill herself if I did not go with her, and so I did – and kept her out of my Lord's washing and ironing – and nobody can deny that, although the charge was high, the linen was well got up.

Hope you are well, Sir, – am, with tears in my eyes,

Yours faithfoolly to command,

Wm Fletcher

P.S. – If you know any Gentleman in want of a Wally – hope for a charakter. I saw your late Swiss Servant in the Galleys at Leghorn for robbing an Inn – he produced your recommendation at his trial.

Byron writes to his publisher, John Murray:

Pisa, December 4, 1821

Dear Sir, – By extracts in the English papers, – in your holy Ally, Galignani's *Messenger*, – I perceive that 'the two greatest examples of human vanity in the "present age" are firstly, "the ex-Emperor Napoleon", and secondly, "his Lordship, etc., the noble poet", meaning your humble servant, poor guiltless I.

Poor Napoleon! he little dreamed to what 'vile comparisons' the turn of the Wheel would reduce him! I cannot help thinking, however, that had our learned brother of the newspaper office seen my very moderate answer to the very scurrile epistle of my radical patron, John Hobhouse, M.P., he would have thought the thermometer of my 'Vanity' reduced to a very decent temperature. By the way you do not happen to know whether Mrs. Fry had commenced her reform of the prisoners at the time when Mr. Hobhouse was in Newgate? there are some of his phrases, and much of his style (in that same letter), which led me to suspect that either she had not, or that he had profited less than the others by her instructions. Last week I sent back the deed of Mr. Moore signed and witnessed. It was inclosed to Mr. Kinnaird with a request to forward it to you. I have also transmitted to him my opinions upon your proposition, etc., etc., but addressed them to himself.

I have got here into a famous old feudal palazzo, on the Arno, large enough for a garrison, with dungeons below and cells in the walls, and so full of Ghosts, that the learned Fletcher (my valet) has begged leave to change his room, and then refused to occupy his new room, because there were more ghosts there than in the other. It is quite true that there are most extraordinary noises (as in all old buildings), which have terrified the servants so as to incommode me extremely. There is one place where people were evidently *walled up*; for there is but one possible passage, *broken* through the wall, and then meant to be closed again upon the inmate. The house belonged to the Lanfranchi family, (the same mentioned by Ugolino in his dream, as his persecutor with

Sismondi), and has had a fierce owner or two in its time. The staircase, etc., is said to have been built by Michel Agnolo [sic]. It is not yet cold enough for a fire. What a climate!

I am, however bothered about these spectres, (as they say the last occupant were, too,) of whom I have as yet seen nothing, nor, indeed, heard [myself]; but all the other ears have been regaled by all kinds of supernatural sounds. The first night I thought I heard an odd noise, but it has not been repeated. I have now been here more than a month.

Yours,
Byron

Lord Byron fell ill in 1824, while in Greece acting as a political negotiator for the Greek Government in their war against Turkey. He was accompanied by a Greek boy acting as his page: Loukas Chalandritsanos, to whom Byron addressed his last poem 'Lines on Completing My Thirty-Sixth Year'. Debilitated from his treatment, which included being bled by his Greek doctor, Byron developed a fever and died after ten days, naming his former lover, Nicolo Giraud, in his will. Lord Byron was mourned in Greece as a national hero.

JEFF WITHERS
born 1804, writing in 1826

These two letters to Jim Hammond have only recently surfaced in the Hammond family papers. They may be the earliest known explicitly gay letters in America. Both men became staid, married pillars of society in the antebellum South.

May 15, 1826
Columbia, South Carolina

Dear Jim:

I got your Letter this morning about 8 o'clock, from the hands of the Bearer. I was sick as the Devil, when the Gentleman entered the Room, and have been so during most of the day. About 1 o'clock I swallowed a huge mass of Epsom Salts – and it will not be hard to imagine that I have been at dirty work since. I feel partially relieved – enough to write a hasty dull letter. I feel some inclination to learn whether you yet sleep in your Shirt-tail, and whether you yet have the extravagant delight of poking and punching a writhing Bedfellow with your long fleshen pole – the exquisite touches of which I have often had the honor of feeling? Let me say unto thee that unless thou changest former habits in this particular, thou wilt be represented by every future Chum as a nuisance. And, I pronounce it, with good reason too. Sir, you roughen the downy Slumbers of your Bedfellow – by such hostile – furious lunges as you are in the habit of making at him – when he is least prepared for defence against the crushing force of a Battering Ram. Without reformation my imagination depicts some awful results for which you will be held accountable – and therefore it is, that I earnestly recommend it. Indeed it is encouraging an assault and battery propensity, which need correction – & uncorrected threatens devastation, horror & bloodshed, etc....

With great respect I am the old
Stud,
Jeff

69

September 24, 1826

My dear Friend,

...Your excellent Letter of 13 June arrived... a few weeks since... the renovation of spirit which follows the appearance of a *friend's* Letter – the diagram of his soul – is like a grateful shower from the cooling fountains of Heaven to reanimate drooping Nature. Whilst your letters are Transcripts of real – existing feeling, and are on that account peculiarly welcome – they at the same time betray too much honesty of purpose not to strike an harmonious chord in my mind. I have only to regret that, honesty of intention and even assiduity in excition [*execution?*] are far from being the uniform agents of our destiney [*sic*] here – However it must, at best, be only an a priori argument for us to settle the condemnation of the world, before we come in actual contact with it. This task is peculiarly appropriate to the acrimony of old age – and perhaps we had as well defer it, under the hope that we may reach a point, when 'twill be all that we can do –

I fancy, Jim, that your *elongated protruberance* – your fleshen pole – your [*two Latin words; indecipherable*] – has captured complete mastery over you – and I really believe, that you are charging over the pine barrens of your locality, braying, like an ass, at every she-male you can discover. I am afraid that you are thus prostituting the 'image of God' and suggest that if you thus blasphemously essay to put on the form of a Jack – in this stead of that noble image – you will share the fate of Nebuchadnazzer of old, I should lament to hear of you feeding upon the dross of the pasture and alarming the country with your vociferations. The day of miracles may not be past, and the flaming excess of your lustful appetite may drag down the vengeance of supernal power. – And you'll 'be damn-d if you don't marry'? – and felt a disposition to set down and gravely detail me the reasons of early marriage. But two favourable ones strike me now – the first is, that Time may grasp love so furiously as totally[*?*] to disfigure his Phiz. The second is, that, like George McDuffie, he may have the hap-hazzard of a broken backbone befal him, which will relieve him from the performance of affectual family-duty – & throw over the brow of his wife, should he chance to get one, a most foreboding gloom – As to the first, you will find many a modest good girl subject to the same inconvenience – and as to the second, it will only superinduce such domestic whirlwinds, as will call into frequent exercise rhetorical displays of impassioned Eloquence, accompanied by appropriate and perfect specimens of those gestures which Nature and feeling suggest. To get children, it is true, fulfills a department of social & natural duty – but to let them starve, or subject them to the alarming hazard of it, violates another of a most important character. This is the dilemma to which I reduce you – choose this day which you will do.

EDWARD FITZGERALD
1809 – 1883

As a young man, Fitzgerald settled in Woodbridge, Suffolk, where he passed a leisurely life surrounded by books, flowers and music. His friends included Thackeray, Fanny Kemble, Tennyson and Carlisle. He married Lucy Barton, the daughter of a Quaker poet, but they soon separated. Among his other achievements, he famously translated The Rubaiyat of Omar Khayyam. *In later life he met a fisherman named Joseph Fletcher, whom he nick-named 'Posh', and whose unsophisticated attitudes attracted him ('… his simplicity of soul, justice of thought, tenderness of nature'); the two men shared a love of the sea, and spent a good deal of time messing about in boats ('…knocking about somewhere outside of Lowestoft'), finally buying a herring lugger together.*

Edward Fitzgerald writes to two friends about his love of the sea:

To W.H. Thompson

10 Marine Terrace, Lowestoft
Nov, 27, 1859

My dear Thompson,

After a Fortnight's Visit to my Sister's (where I caught Cold which flew at once to my Ears, and there hangs) I returned hither, as the nearest Place to go to, and here shall be till Christmas at all Events. I wish to avoid London this winter: and indeed seem almost to have done with it, except for a Day's Business or Sightseeing every now and then. Often should I like to roam about old Cambridge, and hear St Mary's Chimes at Midnight – but – but! Ths Place of course is dull enough: but here's the Old Sea (a dirty Dutch one to be sure) and Sands, and Sailors, a very fine Race of Men, far superior to those in Regent Street. Also the Dutchmen, (an ugly set whom I can't help liking for old Neighbours) come over in their broad Bottoms and take in Water at a Creek along the Shore. But I believe the East Winds get very fierce after Christmas, when the Sea has cooled down. You won't come here, to be sure: or I should be very glad to smoke a Cigar, and have a Chat: and I would take care to have a Fire in your Bedroom this time: a Negligence I was very sorry for in London.

I read, or was told, they wouldn't let old Alfred's Bust *[Tennyson]* into your Trinity. They are right, I think, to let no one in there (as it should be in Westminster Abbey) till a hundred Years are past; when, after too much Admiration (perhaps) and then a Reaction of undue Dis-esteem, Men have settled into some steady Opinion on the subject: supposing always that the Hero survives so long, which of itself goes far to decide the Question. No doubt A.T. will do *that*.

Market-Hill, Woodbridge
Whitmonday *[May 20, 1861]*

My dear George,

I take pleasure in my new little Boat: and last week went with her to Aldbro'; and she 'behaved' very well both going and returning; though, to be sure there was not much to try her Temper. I am so glad of this fine Whit-Monday, when so many Holiday-makers will enjoy theirselves, and so many others make a little money by their Enjoyment. Our 'Rifles' are going to march to Grundisburgh, *manuring* and *skrimmaging* as they go, and also (as the Captain hopes) recruiting. He is a right good little Fellow, I do believe. It is a shame the Gentry hereabout are so indifferent in the Matter: they subscribe next to nothing: and give absolutely nothing in the way of Entertainment or Attention to the Corps. But we are split up into the pettiest possible Squirarchy, who want to make the utmost of their little territory: cut down all the Trees, level all the old Violet Banks, and stop up all the Footways they can. The old pleasant way from Hasketon to Bredfield is now a Desert. I was walking it yesterday and had the pleasure of breaking down and through some Bushes and Hurdles put to block up a fallen Stile. I thought what your Father would have said of it all. And really it is the sad ugliness of our once pleasant Fields that half drives me to the Water where the Power of the Squirarchy stops.

FRYDERICK CHOPIN
1810 – 1849

One of the greatest composers for the piano, Chopin's sexuality appears to have been ambiguous. Though he was invariably surrounded by women and clearly enjoyed a number of liaisons, most notably by the French authoress George Sand, none of them ever drew the sort of devoted and passionate letters from him that his friend Titus Woyciechowski inspired from the composer. Titus was also the dedicatee of Chopin's Variations on a duet from Mozart's Don Giovanni, *'Là ci darem la mano', which translates, 'There we shall take hands, there you will say "I will".' In this letter to Titus, Chopin recalls the première of his First Piano Concerto:*

Warsaw
Saturday 27 March 1830

My dearest friend,

Never have I felt your absence so much as at this moment; you are not here and I have no one to whom I can pour out my feelings. A single glance from you after each of my concerts would have been more to me than all this praise from journalists or people like Elsner, Kurpiński, Soliva and so on. As soon as I got your letter I wanted to describe the first concert, but I was so distracted and occupied with preparations for the second one, which took place on the following Monday, that when I sat down to write I couldn't collect my thoughts. I am still in the same state today, but I won't wait until I can think calmly, as it is time for the post – and calm moments are rare with me Well then, my first concert, although it was sold out and there was not a box or seat to be had three days beforehand, did not make on the general public the impression I thought it would. The first *Allegro* of my concerto, which relatively few could grasp, called forth applause, but it seems to me that people felt they had to show interest ('Ah, something new!') and pretend to be connoisseurs. The *Adagio* and Rondo produced the greatest effect and exclamations of sincere admiration could be heard. But the Pot-pourri on Polish Airs *[Op. 13]* did not in my opinion fully achieve its aim. They applauded because they felt they must show at the end that they had not been bored. Kurpiński discovered fresh beauties in my concerto that evening, but Wiman admitted again that he doesn't know what people see in my first *Allegro*. Ernemann was completely satisfied, but Elsner regretted that the tone of my piano was too woolly and prevented the runs in the bass from being heard. That evening everybody up in the gallery and those standing at the side of the orchestra were satisfied, but the audience in the stalls complained about my playing too quietly – and I would like to have been at 'Cinderella's' *[a Warsaw café]* to hear the arguments that must have raged about me. This is why Monacki, in the *Polish Courier*, after praising me to the skies, particularly for the *Adagio*, ends by advising me to show more *energy*. I considered very carefully where this energy should come from, and at my second concert I played, not on my own piano, but on a Viennese instrument. Diakow, the Russian general, was kind enough to lend me his piano – better than that Hummel one – and at once the audience, which was larger than at the first concert, was satisfied. They applauded straightaway, were delighted that each note sounded like a little pearl and praised me for playing better than at the first concert. When I came forward at the end there were calls for a third concert. The Krakowiak Rondo had an enormous effect and there were four rounds of applause. Kurpiński was sorry I had not played my Fantasia *[on Polish Airs]* on the Viennese instrument and the next day Grzymala expressed the same opinion more strongly in the *Polish Courier*. Elsner's view is that I could only be properly judged after the second concert, but frankly I myself would have preferred to play on my own piano. The general feeling, however, is that the instrument I used was better suited to the hall. You know how the first programme was arranged; well, the second began with Nowakowski's symphony (as a compliment to the composer), then came the first movement, *Allegro*, of the concerto. Bielawski played Bériot's Variations and then came my *Adagio* and Rondo. I began the second half with the Krakowiak Rondo, then Mme Mayer sang in her very best style an aria from Soliva's *Helen and Malvina*. Finally I improvised and greatly pleased the boxes on the first balcony. To be quite frank, I did not improvise in the way I felt inclined to, for it would not have suited that kind of audience. All the same, I am surprised that the Adagio made such a general impression: wherever I go they speak of nothing else. You have of course had all the newspapers, or at least the main ones, and you can confirm that everyone was delighted. Mlle de Moriolles sent me a laurel wreath and today somebody else sent me a poem. Orlowski has written mazurkas and waltzes on themes from my concerto, and Sennewald, Brzezina's partner, has asked for my portrait [*to have it engraved and sold*], but I could not allow that – it would be going too far: I have no desire to see myself used for wrapping up butter, which is what happened to Lelewel's portrait.

I will send you my portrait as soon as I possibly can; you want it and shall have it, but no one else. Well, I might give it to one other person, but not before you, who are dearest to me. No one but myself has read your letter. Now, as always, I carry your letters about with me. In May, when I go for a walk outside the town, thinking of my approaching journey, what a joy it will be to take out your letter and learn again beyond doubt that you love me; or at least I can look at the hand and writing of one to whom I am absolutely devoted! They want me to give another concert but I have no desire to do so. You can't imagine 11 what a torture the three days before a public appearance are to me. Besides, I shall be finishing the first *Allegro* of my second concerto before the holidays – that's why I shall wait until after the holidays before giving a third concert, although I know that even at this moment I could have a much larger audience, for the people in high society have not heard me often. Among the voices from the stalls, at my last concert, calling for a third one, there was one shouting: 'In the Town Hall!' so loudly that I heard it on the stage. But I doubt whether I shall take any notice, and if I do give a concert it will certainly be at the theatre. It's not a question of making money – the theatre did not bring in much, for the box-office clerk had a free hand and took charge of everything. After deducting expenses I did not get five thousand [*zlotys*] from both concerts, although, as Dmuszewski reminded me, for a concert with a pianist the audience had never been so large as at my first concert – and – even more so at the second. What concerns me most is the fact that at the Town Hall I should have just the same difficulties and yet not make a very much better impression by my playing. I could not play to suit everyone and should have to choose between the aristocracy and the townsfolk. If and when I do play, I still feel:

> Unborn is he for whom mankind
> Nought but words of praise can find.

Dobrzyński looks askance at me because I did not select his symphony; Mme Wodzińska is furious that I did not reserve her a box... and so on.

HERMAN MELVILLE
1819 – 1891

The writer Herman Melville, most famous for his sea adventures Moby Dick *and* Billy Budd, *fell in love with novelist Nathaniel Hawthorne (1804–1864) between 1850 and 1851, when they were neighbours in Pittsfield. Melville had bought a farm there, 'Arrowhead', after his marriage. Hawthorne, too, was married. Fifteen years older than Melville, he was extraordinarily handsome and, like Melville, had attractive feminine qualities. Melville wrote: 'A man of a deep and noble nature has seized me in this seclusion. His wild, witch-voice rings through me.' On another occasion he confided: 'This "all" feeling... you must often have felt it, lying on the grass on a warm summer's day. Your legs seem to send out shoots into the earth. Your hair feels like leaves upon your head! This is the "all" feeling...'*

Melville, fascinated by his new companion, writes to his literary friend Duyckinck:

Pittsfield, Wednesday, 1851

My dear Duyckinck... After a long procrastination I went down to see Mr. Hawthorne a couple of weeks ago. I found him, of course, buried in snow; and the delightful scenery about him all wrapped up and tucked away under a napkin as it were. He was to have made me a day's visit, and I had promised myself much pleasure in getting him up in my snug room here, and discussing the universe with a bottle of brandy and cigars. But he has not been able to come, owing to sickness in his family – or else he's up to the lips in the *Universe* again.

By the way, I have recently read his *Twice Told Tales* (I hadn't read but a few of them before). I think they far exceed the 'Mosses'. They are, I fancy, an earlier vintage from his vine. Some of those sketches are wonderfully subtle. Their deeper meanings are worthy of a Brahmin. Still there is something lacking – a good deal lacking to the plump sphericality of the man. What is that? He doesn't patronise the butcher – he needs roast-beef, done rare.

Nevertheless, for one, I regard Hawthorne (in his books) as evincing a quality of genius immensely loftier, and more profound, too, than any other American has shown hitherto in the printed form. Irving is a grasshopper to him – putting the souls of the two men together, I mean. But I must close...

Truly yours,
H. Melville

WALT WHITMAN
1819 – 1892

One of America's greatest poets, Whitman was raised and educated in Brooklyn though his most lasting education was on his own where he read the great writers on his own initiative. His experiences as a volunteer nurse during the Civil War had a lasting effect on him and he aged considerably during this time. The transformation from the young poet portrayed in his Leaves of Grass *of 1951 to the white haired 44-year-old is notable. Though poor for much of his life – he worked in a variety of minor posts in Washington – he had a varied and devoted following. Among the many young men to whom he became attached, Peter Doyle drew from him some of the most affectionate letters. He refers to Doyle's ailment, a skin disease, which had been provoking suicidal thoughts in the young man.*

Brooklyn, N. Y.
Saturday evening – 21 August 1869

Dear Pete –

I have been very sick the last three days – I don't know what to call it – it makes me prostrated & deathly weak, & little use of my limbs. I have thought of you, my darling boy, very much of the time. I have not been out of the house since the first day after my arrival. I had a pleasant journey through on the cars Wednesday afternoon & night – felt quite well then. My Mother & folks are all well. We are in our new house – we occupy part & rent out part. I have a nice room, where I now sit writing this. It is the latter part of the afternoon. I feel better the last hour or so. It has been extremely hot here the last two days – I see it has been so in Washington too. I hope I shall get out soon. I hanker to get out doors, & down the bay.

And now, dear Pete, for yourself. How is it with you, dearest boy – and is there any thing different with the face? Dear Pete, you must forgive me for being so cold the last day & evening. I was unspeakably shocked and repelled from you by that talk & proposition of yours – you know what – there by the fountain. It seemed indeed to me, (for I will talk out plainly to you, dearest comrade,) that the one I loved, and who had always been so manly & sensible, was gone, & a fool &

intentional murderer stood in his place. I spoke so sternly & cutting. (Though I see now that my words might have appeared to have a certain other meaning, which I didn't dream of, insulting to you, never for one moment in my thoughts.) But I will say no more of this – for I know such thoughts must have come when you was not yourself, but in a moment of derangement – & have passed away like a bad dream.

Dearest boy, I have not a doubt that you will get well, and entirely well – & we will one day look back on these drawbacks & sufferings as things long past. The extreme cases of that malady, (as I told you before) are persons that have a very deeply diseased blood, probably with syphilis in it, inherited from parentage, & confirmed by themselves – so they have no foundation to build on. You are of healthy stock, with a sound constitution, & good blood – & I know it is impossible for it to continue long. My darling, if you are not well when I come back I will get a good room or two in some quiet place, (or out of Washington, perhaps in Baltimore,) and we will live together, & devote ourselves altogether to the job of curing you, & rooting the cursed thing out entirely, & making you stronger & healthier than ever, I have had this in my mind before, but never broached it to you. I could go on with my work in the Attorney General's office just the same – & we would see that your mother should have a small sum every week to keep the pot a-boiling at home.

Dear comrade, I think of you very often. My love for you is indestructible, & since that night & morning has returned more than before.

Dear Pete, dear son, my darling boy, my young & loving brother, don't let the devil put such thoughts in your mind again – wickedness unspeakable – murder, death & disgrace here, & hell's agonies hereafter – Then what would it be afterward to the mother? What to me? –

Pete, I send you some money, by Adam's Express – you use it, dearest son, & when it is gone, you shall have some more, for I have plenty.

I will write again before long – give my love to Johnny Lee, my dear darling boy, I love him truly – (let him read these three last lines) – Dear Pete, *remember* –

Walt

JOHN ADDINGTON SYMONDS
1840 – 1893

The son of a doctor, J. A. Symonds spent much of his life in Europe because of his consumption. He did much to popularise Italian culture and published a great number of books on the subject of Italian art. One of his other preoccupations was the homosexual psyche and he corresponded frequently with Edward Carpenter, one of the earliest commentators on the subject.

<u>Private</u>

Am Hof Davos Platz
29 December 1892

My dear Carpenter

Thank you much for your letter & the promise of your book.

I will send you my last little book in return. It is called *In the Key of Blue*. I fear you will not find much in it. Look at 'Platonic Love', 'Clifton', & the first Essay.

I am so glad that H. Ellis has told you about our project. I never saw him. But I like his way of corresponding on this subject. And I need somebody of medical importance to collaborate with. Alone, I could make but little effect – the effect of an eccentric.

We are agreed enough upon fundamental points. The only difference is that he is too much inclined to stick to the neuropathical theory of explanation. But I am whittling that away to a minimum. And I don't think it politic to break off from the traditional line of analysis, which has been going rapidly forward in Europe for the last 20 years upon the psychiatric theory. Each new book reduces the conception of neurotic disease.

I mean to introduce a new feature into the discussion, by giving a complete account of homosexual love in ancient Greece. I wrote this some time ago, & had 10 copies of it privately printed. If you like to see it, I will lend you one of my two remaining copies. I should indeed value a word from you about it.

All the foreign investigators from Moreau & Casper to Moll, are totally ignorant of Greek Customs. Yet it is here that the phenomenon has to be studied from a different point of view from that of psycho-pathology. Here we are forced to recognise that one of the foremost races in civilization not only tolerated passionate comradeship, but also utilised it for high social and military purpose.

(By the way, in the book I send you, you will find an essay on the subject.)

You raise a very interesting question with regard to physiological grounds for this passion. I have no doubt myself that the absorption of semen implies a real modification of the physique of the person who absorbs it, & that, in these homosexual relations, this constitutes an important basis for subsequent conditions – both spiritual & corporeal.

It is a pity that we cannot write freely on the topic. But when we meet, I will communicate to you facts which prove beyond all doubt to my mind that the most beneficent results, as regards health and nervous energy, accrue from the sexual relation between men: also, that when they are carried on with true affection, through a period of years, both comrades become united in a way which would be otherwise quite inexplicable.

The fact appears to me proved. The explanation of it I cannot give, & I do not expect it to be given yet. Sex has been unaccountably neglected. Its physiological & psychological relations even in the connection between man & woman are not understood. We have no theory which is worth anything upon the differentiation of the sexes, to begin with. In fact, a science of what is the central function of human beings remains to be sought.

This, I take it, is very much due to physiologists, assuming that sexual instincts follow the build of the sexual organs; & that when they do not, the phenomenon is criminal or morbid. In fact, it is due to science at this point being still clogged with religious & legal presuppositions.

Any good book upon homosexual passions advances the sound method of induction, out of which may possibly be wrought in the future a sound theory of sex in general. The first thing is to force people to see that the passions in question have their justification in nature.

My hope has always been that eventually a new chivalry, i.e. a second elevated form of human love, will emerge & take its place for the service of mankind by the side of that other which was wrought out in the Middle Ages.

It will be complementary, by no means prejudicial to the elder & more commonly acceptable. It will engage a different type of individual in different spheres of energy – aims answering to those of monastic labour in common or of military self-devotion to duty taking here the place of domestic cares & procreative utility.

How far away the dream seems! And yet I see in human nature stuff neglected, ever-present – parish and outcast now – from which I am as certain as that I live, such a chivalry could arise.

Whitman, in *Calamus*, seemed to strike the key-note. And though he repudiated (in a very notable letter to myself) the deductions which have logically to be drawn from *Calamus*, his work will remain infinitely helpful.

South-Sea Idylls. C. W. Stoddard. Boston. James R. Osgood. 1873. I got mine from Sampson Low, I think, through Nutt 270 Strand. If you cannot get a copy, let me hear, & I will send you mine. It was suppressed once in America.

Now, dear friend, farewell. I put 'Private' on this letter, qui habent sua fata epistolare.

Yours in affection
JAS

Davos
5 February 1893

My dear Carpenter

I did send you my Problem in Greek Ethics, & will now send you the Modern Problem – which please to keep if you care. Since the latter was written, Moll & Schrenck-Notzing have done a great deal to whittle down the theory of 'erbliche Belastung' *[hereditary taint]*. My elaborate polemic against Krafft-Ebing is hardly required now.

Your notes are very interesting & valuable. Percy's love-letter is quite charming, & the silhouette of the Sheffield show-boy delightful.

What the guardsman said to your friend accords with what I know about military prostitution. I made acquaintance last autumn in Venice with a Corporal of the 2d Life Guards who was travelling with a man I knew. He gave me a great deal of information. But it all pointed to the mercantile aspect of the matter. However, he said that some men 'listed on purpose to indulge their propensities'. An Italian Colonel told me the same thing – i.e. that young men of the best families, after serving as volunteers, or in the natural course of conscription, would sometimes remain on in the ranks with a view to the opportunities afforded by barracks.

Referring to what you stated as to Case H, the only boy among 6 sisters, I have wondered whether cases of this sort do not support Ulrich's physiological hypothesis: as though the combination of the parents tended to female sexuality in the differentiation of the offspring, so that when a male came he was feminine in temperament.

I know a decided Invert, who grew up with 3 sisters. But his parents had produced before him 2 still-born males, & a third who died in infancy of acute inflammation of the brain. The sisters normal, & all married.

This will not prove much, however. I know two Ducal families in which there is Sexual Inversion. One is Somerset, where males & females are pretty equally distributed. The name of the other I will not mention. But here also males & females occur in balanced quantities. The eldest son, the Duke, was a man much given to women. The second married a cousin of mine, & died after the birth of their first child, a boy. The third is an invert of marked quality. He is a great friend of mine, & tells me that he thinks he inherited his temperament from a Ducal great uncle of a different race.

I wish the medical psychologists would study the phenomenon from this point of view. If only it had fallen into the hands of Fr. Galton!

Did you get a copy of *South Sea Idylls?*

Apropos of yr friend the engine driver – I must tell you how much I admire that passage in *Toward Democracy* (pp 140-143).

Yrs affectly

J.A.S.

PYOTR ILYICH TCHAIKOVSKY
1840–1893

One of the world's greatest composers, Tchaikovsky's homosexuality was a profound influence on his creative life. The heroine of his greatest opera Eugene Onegin, *Tatyana, perfectly mirrors the typical uncertainties and agonies of the homosexual in an unsympathetic society: her love for a man whose rejection of her is brutal needs little 'translation'. It is now widely thought that Tchaikovsky committed suicide to prevent a scandal as the result of his feelings for a young Russian aristocrat. It is an appalling tale and adds an intensity to the autobiographical elements of his already emotionally rich music.*

Why do I not visit Turgenev? The question provokes me to give a very thorough and detailed answer. All my life I have been a martyr to the relationships which I have been obliged to keep up with people. I am an unsociable person by nature. I have always found knowing people and meeting new people a source of acute mental strain. I even find it difficult to explain what the real nature of the strain is. Perhaps it is shyness taken to the point of mania, perhaps it is the utter and complete absence of any need for sociability, perhaps it is the misguided fear of appearing other than I am, perhaps it is the inability to say what I don't think without forcing myself to it (and without this ability one will never get to know anybody), in short I do not know what it is but what I do know is that, when my situation did not permit me to avoid meeting people, I did meet them, pretended that I enjoyed it, was compelled by sheer necessity to act out my part (because if one lives in society there is no possibility of avoiding this), and suffered agonies. Only God knows what I went through. I am so happy and relaxed now precisely because I can, at least here and in the country, live without seeing anybody apart from those with whom I can be myself. Never in my life have I made so much as a move to get to know somebody or other interesting. And if it has happened of its own accord, by force of circumstances, all it has brought me has been disappointment, sadness, and exhaustion. What I mean is, in broader terms, this: in my opinion one can enjoy someone else's company only when, after knowing them and sharing their interests (especially family interests) for many years, one can be oneself with them. Without this, any form of association is a burden and my mental make-up is such that it is a burden which I am unable to bear. That is why I do not go to see Turgenev or anybody else. There are plenty of people I could go to see here. Saint-Saëns is here and when he was in Moscow he made me promise that whenever I was in Paris I would visit him. Anybody else in my position would have got to know all the people to do with music here. And I very much regret not having done so – I miss a lot because of my unsociability. How I have struggled with this failing of mine and how much I have suffered in the battle with my peculiar character! What a torment it has been! How hard I have worked at trying to change myself! But it does not worry me now. I have finally convinced myself that there is no point in keeping trying to re-educate myself. Turgenev has several times expressed a sympathetic interest in my music. Viardot has sung some of my songs; so it would seem that I ought to have gone to see them and it would probably even have been useful. But I am now reconciled to the notion that my unsociability paralyses my chances of success and have stopped worrying about it altogether. I have been very happy since I have been able to hide away in my burrow where I can always be myself; I have been happy since books and music have been my constant and almost my only companions. As to actually knowing famous people, my experience has led me to stumble upon the truth that their books and their music are more interesting than they are themselves.

I have been walking round Paris like quite another man, like an idle flâneur in fact, and perhaps this is why all the love which I have nurtured for this city over the years is making itself felt with the force which it used to have in my youth. This process has, incidentally, been aided by another circumstance: my *Tempest* has been announced for one of the Châtelet concerts. Meeting my name on the advertising pillars and in the windows of music shops has made me feel at home in Paris.

It will be an entirely new feeling for me to hear one of my own works in the audience, which will have no suspicion of my presence. This feeling could be remarkably pleasant if the performance turns out to be good. As far as success or failure is concerned, I assure you that I am not even thinking about it, so convinced am I in advance of its failure. The French public has got thoroughly stuck in a musical rut, and if it chooses to recognise its own native musicians only many years after their death, what can foreigners expect. I will not be at all surprised and will be very little hurt by failure: I am an old hand at this.

The torments I have gone through are the clearest possible proof that I should not live anywhere but in the country. Even listening to my own works, which previously gave me the greatest pleasure, has become nothing but a source of agony. One would have thought that the conditions under which I heard *The Tempest* would have assured my complete tranquillity. Not at all. From the morning onwards, and right up to the opening chords, my agitation was crescendo all the time and when they started playing I was in such a state of perturbation that I thought I would die, right there, on the spot. And I was agitated because for some time every fresh hearing of one of my works, whatever it may be, has been accompanied by the most acute sense of disappointment in myself. As if on purpose, they played Mendelssohn's 'Reformation' Symphony before *The Tempest*; though it did move me very much, I was constantly astonished by his marvellous craftsmanship. I lack craftsmanship. I still write like a promising young man of whom much can be expected but who gives very little. What surprises me most of all is that my orchestra sounds so bad. Of course my reason tells me that I am rather exaggerating my faults, but that is small consolation. *The Tempest* was performed not badly at all, although it was not first-rate either. The tempi were absolutely right. I thought that the musicians played diligently but without enthusiasm or love. One of them (a cellist), whom for some reason I could not take my eyes off, was smiling and looked as if he was exchanging glances with someone, as if to say, 'Forgive us for offering you such strange fare, but it isn't our fault: they order us to play and we play!' When the final chords had been played, reasonably warm applause broke out, then it was as if another round was in preparation, but at this point there were three or four very loud whistles, whereupon the hall was filled with cries of 'Oh! Oh!', signifying a well-meant protest against the hissing, and then the hall fell silent. I withstood all this without any particular feelings of hurt, but I was devastated by the thought that *The Tempest*, which I have grown used to regarding as my most brilliant composition, is in fact so worthless! I left immediately. The weather was wonderful and I walked for about two hours without stopping, after which I went home and wrote a note to Colonne in which I lied that I had only been in Paris for one day and therefore could not be there in person. The note expresses sincere gratitude, and indeed, he had learnt *The Tempest* very well. After that I felt notably calmer. I have adjusted to this situation by deciding that after the opera and the suite I will, at last, write a model symphonic work. And so it seems that until I draw my last breath I will only strive for mastery and never attain it.

SIR ARTHUR SULLIVAN
1842 – 1900

Arthur Seymour Sullivan was born in London into a musical family. By the age of eight years he was an accomplished player of all the instruments in his father's band. In 1871 he met dramatic critic and librettist W.S. Gilbert. Together they wrote operettas (e.g. HMS Pinafore, The Mikado, The Yeomen of the Guard, The Pirates of Penzance) *for which the Savoy Theatre was especially built by Richard D'Oyly Carte. Sullivan's homosexuality was very discreet, but, though this has been little discussed by music historians, some think it might have led to the break-up of his partnership with W.S. Gilbert.*

Here, at the age of eighteen, he writes home from Leipzig, where he is studying piano, conducting and composition:

October 31, 1860

Leipzig

My great hobby is still conducting. I have been told by many of the masters here that I was born to be a conductor and consequently have been educating myself to a high degree in that branch of the art. If I can only once obtain an opportunity to show what I can do in that way I feel confident of my success afterwards. Do not mistake this for conceit... but I am getting of an age now when I shall be obliged to have confidence in myself and my own resources. I often try to think what would have become of me had I never come to Germany. In England there was very little more for me to learn. I had heard and knew well almost all the small stock of music which is ever performed in London (and it is *very* little compared to what one hears here). I should have made very little improvement in pianoforte playing, whereas now, thanks to Messrs. Moscheles and Plaidy, I am a tolerably decent player... Besides increasing and maturing my judgment of music it has taught me how good works ought to be done. They have no idea in England of making the orchestras play with that degree of light and shade to which they have attained here, and that is what I aim at – to bring the English orchestra to the same perfection as the Continental ones, and to even still greater, for the power and tone of ours are much greater than the foreign.

Sullivan was a little wry about English audiences...

If something does not please them (tickle their ears) the first time they hear it they throw it aside and will not have anything more to do with it, forgetting that really good music is seldom appreciated by one the first time of hearing, but that it grows on one and one sees its beauties gradually. Take Beethoven, for instance. His fifth symphony was poohpooh'd and laughed at when it was first tried at the Philharmonic; Carl, M. von Weber said of his eighth (or seventh) that the composer was fit for the madhouse. The Choral Symphony is only just now beginning to be *understood* in England. And yet what do we think of Beethoven now?

HENRY JAMES
1843 – 1916

The great novelist Henry James was an influence on succeeding generations of writers, with such novels as Washington Square, The Bostonians *and* The Turn of the Screw.

    Born in New York, he actually spent the greater part of his life in England. In middle age he fell in love with a young, and only moderately successful, sculptor named Hendrik Andersen, to whom James wrote adoring letters: 'I hold you close'; 'I feel, my dear boy, my arms around you'; 'The sense that I can't help you, see you, talk to you, touch you, hold you close and long, or do anything to make you rest on me – this torments me, dearest boy, makes me ache for you and for myself. I wish I could go to Rome, and put my hands on you (Oh, how lovingly I should lay them)'.

    James was also great friends with Hugh Walpole, who was a little possessive (once writing of James's friendship with one Jocelyn Persse: 'Believe it or not, Henry James was madly in love with him.') However, Henry James enjoyed Walpole's youthful zest for living…

To Hugh Walpole

Reform Club, Pall Mall, S.W.
May 19th, 1912

    …Your letter greatly moves and regales me. Fully do I enter into your joy of sequestration, and your bliss of removal from this scene of heated turmoil and dusty despair – which, however, re-awaits you! Never mind; sink up to your neck into the brimming basin of nature and peace, and teach yourself – by which I mean let your grandmother teach you – that with each revolving year you will need and make more piously these precious sacrifices to Pan and the Muses. History eternally repeats itself, and I remember well how in the old London years (of *my* old London – *this* isn't that one) I used to clutch at these chances of obscure flight and at the possession, less frustrated, of my soul, my sense and my hours. So keep it up; I miss you, little as I see you even when here (for I *feel* you more than I see you;) but I surrender you at whatever cost to the beneficent powers. Therefore I rejoice in the getting on of your work – how splendidly copious your flow; and am much interested in what you tell me of your readings and your literary emotions. These latter indeed – or some of them, as you express them, I don't think I fully share. At least when you ask me if I don't feel Dostoieffsky's 'mad jumble, that flings things down in a heap', nearer truth and beauty than the picking and composing that you instance in Stevenson, I reply with emphasis that I feel nothing of the sort, and that the older I grow and the more I *go* the more sacred to me do picking and composing become – though I naturally don't limit myself to Stevenson's *kind* of the same. Don't let any one persuade you – there are plenty of ignorant and fatuous duffers to try to do it – that strenuous selection and comparison are not the very essence of art, and that Form *is* [*not*] substance to that degree that there is absolutely no substance without it. Form alone *takes*, and holds and preserves, substance – saves it from the welter of helpless verbiage that we swim in as in a sea of tasteless tepid pudding, and that makes one ashamed of an art capable of such degradations. Tolstoi and D. are fluid puddings, though not tasteless, because the amount of their own minds and souls in solution in the broth gives it savour and flavour, thanks to the strong, rank quality of their genius and their experience. But there are all sorts of things to be said of them, and in particular that we see how great a vice is their lack of composition, their defiance of economy and architecture, directly they are emulated and imitated; *then*, as subjects of emulation, models, they quite give themselves away. There is nothing so deplorable as a work of art with a *leak* in its interest; and there is no such leak of interest as through commonness of form. Its opposite, the *found* (because the sought-for) form is the absolute citadel and tabernacle of interest. But what a lecture I am reading you – though a very imperfect one – which you have drawn upon yourself (as moreover it was quite right you should.) But no matter – I shall go for you again – as soon as I find you in a lone corner...

Well, dearest Hugh, love me a little better (if you *can*) for this letter, for I am ever so fondly and faithfully yours,

Henry James

Henry James writes to a novelist friend, Howard Sturgis:

To Howard Sturgis

Lamb House, Rye
August 17th, 1911

Beloved creature!

As if I hadn't mainly spent my time since my return here (a week ago yesterday) in writhing and squirming for very shame at having left your several, or at least your generously two or three last, exquisite outpourings unanswered. But I had long before sailing from là-bas, dearest Howard, and especially during the final throes and exhaustions, been utterly overturned by the savage heat and drought of a summer that had set in furiously the very last of May, going crescendo all that time – and of which I am finding here (so far as the sky of brass and the earth of cinders is concerned) so admirable an imitation. I have shown you often enough, I think, how much more I have in me of the polar bear than of the salamander – and in fine, at the time I last heard from you, pen, ink and paper had dropped from my perspiring grasp (though while in the grasp they had never felt more adhesively sticky,) and I had become a mere prostrate, panting, liquefying mass, wailing to be removed. I *was* removed – at the date I mention – pressing your supreme benediction (in the form of eight sheets of lovely 'stamped paper', as they say in the U.S.) to my heaving bosom; but only to less sustaining and refreshing conditions than I had hoped for here. You will understand how some of these – in this seamed and cracked and blasted and distracted country – strike me; and perhaps even a little how I seem to myself to have been transferred simply from one sizzling grid-iron to another – at a time when my further toleration of grid-irons had reached its lowest ebb. *Such* a pile of waiting letters greeted me here – most of them pushing in with an indecency of clamour before *your* dear delicate signal. But it is always of you, dear and delicate and supremely interesting, that I have been thinking, and here is just a poor palpitating stopgap of a reply. Don't take it amiss of my wise affection if I tell you that I am heartily glad you are going to Scotland. Go, *go*, and stay as long as you ever can – it's the sort of thing exactly that will do you a world of good. I am to go there, I believe, next month, to stay four or five days with John Cadwalader – and eke with Minnie of that ilk (or more or less,) in Forfarshire – but that will probably be lateish in the month; and before I go you will have come back from the Eshers and I have returned from a visit of a few days which I expect to embark upon on Saturday next. Then, when we are gathered in, no power on earth will prevent me from throwing myself on your bosom.

Forgive meanwhile the vulgar sufficiency and banality of my advice, above, as to what will 'do you good' – loathsome expression! But one grasps in one's haste the cheapest current coin. I commend myself strongly to the gentlest (no, that's not the word – say the firmest even while the fairest) of Williams, and am yours, dearest Howard, ever so yearningly.

Henry James

OSCAR WILDE
1854 – 1900

The story of Oscar Wilde's trial and imprisonment, followed by his exile in France makes for painful reading. The facts are well known and the awful irony that the instrument of his fall was none other than the father of his lover Lord Alfred Douglas ('Bosie') merely adds to the sadness of the events. 'De Profundis' is a long and moving letter written during Wilde's incarceration in Reading prison. It was sent initially to Wilde's friend Robbie Ross who copied it and then sent it to Douglas who destroyed it after reading only a few pages – it must have been a painful experience seeing the bare facts of their relationship and Douglas's treatment of Wilde so exposed. The copy was deposited in the British Library where it was finally opened in 1960. The extract that follows comprises the opening and the close. The central section – many thousands of words – is a meditation on morality and the events which lead to the dissolution of a talent of extraordinary scale and range. It is one of the most classic 'gay letters' ever penned.

DE PROFUNDIS
'Epistola: In Carcere et Vinculis'

H.M. Prison
Reading

[January - March 1897]

Dear Bosie,

After long and fruitless waiting I have determined to write to you myself, as much for your sake as for mine, as I would not like to think that I had passed through two long years of imprisonment without ever having received a single line from you, or any news or message even, except such as gave me pain.

Our ill-fated and most lamentable friendship has ended in ruin and public infamy for me, yet the memory of our ancient affection is often with me, and the thought that loathing, bitterness and contempt should for ever take that place in my heart once held by love is very sad to me: and you yourself will, I think, feel in your heart that to write to me as I lie in the loneliness of prison-life is better than to publish my letters without my permission or to dedicate poems to me unasked, though the world will know nothing of whatever words of grief or passion, of remorse or indifference you may choose to send as your answer or your appeal.

I have no doubt that in this letter in which I have to write of your life and of mine, of the past and of the future, of sweet things changed to bitterness and of bitter things that may be turned into joy, there will be much that will wound your vanity to the quick. If it prove so, read the letter over and over again till it kills your vanity. If you find in it something of which you feel that you are unjustly accused, remember that one should be thankful that there is any fault of which one can be unjustly accused. If there be in it one single passage that brings tears to your eyes, weep as we weep in prison where the day no less than the night is set apart for tears. It is the only thing that can save you. If you go complaining to your mother, as you did with reference to the scorn of you I displayed in my letter to Robbie, so that she may flatter and soothe you back into self-complacency or conceit, you will be completely lost. If you find one false excuse for yourself, you will soon find a hundred, and be just what you were before. Do you still say, as you said to Robbie in your answer, that I 'attribute unworthy motives' to you? Ah! you had no motives in life. You had appetites merely. A motive is an intellectual aim. That you were 'very young' when our friendship began? Your defect was not that you knew so·little about life, but that you knew so much. The morning dawn of boyhood with its delicate bloom, its clear pure light, its joy of innocence and expectation you had left far behind. With very swift and running feet you had passed from Romance to Realism. The gutter and the things that live in it had begun to fascinate you. That was the origin of the trouble in which you sought my aid, and I, so unwisely according to the wisdom of this world, out of pity and kindness gave it to you. You must read this letter right through, though each word may become to you as the fire or knife of the surgeon that makes the delicate flesh burn or bleed. Remember that the fool in the eyes of the gods and the fool in the eyes of man are very different. One who is entirely ignorant of the modes of

Art in its revolution or the moods of thought in its progress, of the pomp of the Latin line or the richer music of the vowelled Greek, of Tuscan sculpture or Elizabethan song may yet be of the very sweetest wisdom. The real fool, such as the gods mock or mar, is he who does not know himself. I was such a one too long. You have been such a one too long. Be so no more. Do not be afraid. The supreme vice is shallowness. Everything that is realized is right. Remember also that whatever is misery to you to read, is still greater misery to me to set down. To you the Unseen Powers have been very good. They have permitted you to see the strange and tragic shapes of Life as one sees shadows in a crystal. The head of Medusa that turns living men to stone, you have been allowed to look at in a mirror merely. You yourself have walked free among the flowers. From me the beautiful world of colour and motion has been taken away.

I will begin by telling you that I blame myself terribly. As I sit here in this dark cell in convict clothes, a disgraced and ruined man, I blame myself. In the perturbed and fitful nights of anguish, in the long monotonous days of pain, it is myself I blame. I blame myself for allowing an unintellectual friendship, a friendship whose primary aim was not the creation and contemplation of beautiful things, to entirely dominate my life. From the very first there was too wide a gap between us. You had been idle at your school, worse than idle at your university. You did not realise that an artist, and especially such an artist as I am, one, that is to say, the quality of whose work depends on the intensification of personality, requires for the development of his art the companionship of ideas, an intellectual atmosphere, quiet, peace, and solitude. You admired my work when it was finished: you enjoyed the brilliant successes of my first nights, and the brilliant banquets that followed them: you were proud, and quite naturally so, of being the intimate friend of an artist so distinguished: but you could not understand the conditions requisite for the production of artistic work. I am not speaking in phrases of rhetorical exaggeration but in terms of absolute truth to actual fact when I remind you that during the whole time we were together I never wrote one single line. Whether at Torquay, Goring,

London, Florence, or elsewhere, my life, as long as you were by my side, was entirely sterile and uncreative. And with but few intervals you were, I regret to say, by my side always.

I remember, for instance, in September '93, to select merely one instance out of many, taking a set of chambers, purely in order to work undisturbed, as I had broken my contract with John Hare for whom I had promised to write a play, and who was pressing me on the subject. During the first week you kept away. We had, not unnaturally indeed, differed on the question of the artistic value of your translation of *Salome*, so you contented yourself with sending me foolish letters on the subject. In that week I wrote and completed in every detail, as it was ultimately performed, the first act of *An Ideal Husband*. The second week you returned and my work practically had to be given up. I arrived at St James's Place every morning at 11.30, in order to have the opportunity of thinking and writing without the interruptions inseparable from my own household, quiet and peaceful as that household was. But the attempt was vain. At twelve o'clock you drove up, and stayed smoking cigarettes and chattering till 1.30, when I had to take you out to luncheon at the Café Royal or the Berkeley. Luncheon with its *liqueurs* lasted usually till 3.30. For an hour you retired to White's. At tea-time you appeared again, and stayed till it was time to dress for dinner. You dined with me either at the Savoy or at Tite Street. We did not separate as a rule till after midnight, as supper at Willis's had to wind up the entrancing day. That was my life for those three months, every single day, except during the four days when you went abroad. I then, of course, had to go over to Calais to fetch you back. For one of my nature and temperament it was a position at once grotesque and tragic.

You surely must realise that now? You must see now that your incapacity of being alone: your nature so exigent in its persistent claim on the attention and time of others: your lack of any power of sustained intellectual concentration: the unfortunate accident – for I like to think it was no more – that you had not yet been able to acquire the 'Oxford temper' in intellectual matters, never, I mean, been one who could play gracefully with ideas but had arrived at violence of opinion merely – that all these things, combined with the fact that your desires and interests were in Life not in Art, were as destructive to your own progress in culture as they were to my work as an artist? When I compare my friendship with you to my friendship with such still younger men as John Gray and Pierre Louÿs I feel ashamed. My real life, my higher life was with them and such as they.

Of the appalling results of my friendship with you I don't speak at present. I am thinking merely of its quality while it lasted. It was intellectually degrading to me. You had the rudiments of an artistic temperament in its germ. But I met you either too late or too soon, I don't know which. When you were away I was all right. The moment, in the early December of the year to which I have been alluding, I had succeeded in inducing your mother to send you out of England, I collected again the torn and ravelled web of my imagination, got my life back into my own hands, and not merely finished the three remaining acts of *An Ideal Husband*, but conceived and had almost completed two other plays of a completely different type, the *Florentine Tragedy* and *La Sainte Courtisane*, when suddenly, unbidden, unwelcome, and under circumstances fatal to my happiness you returned. The two works left then imperfect I was unable to take up again. The mood that created them I could never recover. You now, having yourself published a volume of verse, will be able to recognise the truth of everything I have said here. Whether you can or not it remains as a hideous truth in the very heart of our friendship. While you were with me you were the absolute ruin of my Art, and in allowing you to stand persistently between Art and myself I give to myself shame and blame in the fullest degree. You couldn't know, you couldn't understand, you couldn't appreciate. I had no right to expect it of you at all. Your interests were merely in your meals and moods. Your desires were simply for amusements, for ordinary or less ordinary! pleasures. They were what your temperament needed, or thought it needed for the moment. I should have forbidden you my house and my chambers except when I specially invited you. I blame myself without reserve for my weakness. It was merely weakness. One halfhour with Art was always more to me than a cycle with you. Nothing really at any period of my life was ever of the smallest importance to me compared with Art. But in the case of an artist, weakness is nothing less than a crime, when it is a weakness that paralyses the imagination.

I blame myself again for having allowed you to bring me to utter and discreditable financial ruin. I remember one morning in the early October of '92 sitting in the yellowing woods at Bracknell with your mother. At that time I knew very little of your real nature. I had stayed from a Saturday to Monday with you at Oxford. You had stayed with me at Cromer for ten days and played golf. The conversation turned on you, and your mother began to speak to me about your character. She told me of your two chief faults, your vanity, and your being, as she termed it, *'all wrong about money'*. I have a distinct recollection of how I laughed. I had no idea that the first would bring me to prison, and the second to bankruptcy. I thought vanity a sort of graceful flower for a young man to wear; as for extravagance – for I thought she meant no more than extravagance – the virtues of prudence and thrift were not in my own nature or my own race. But before our friendship was one month older I began to see what your mother really meant. Your insistence on a life of reckless profusion: your incessant demands for money: your claim that all your pleasures should be paid for by me whether I was with you or not: brought me after some time into serious monetary difficulties, and what made the extravagances to me at any rate so monotonously uninteresting, as your persistent grasp on my life grew stronger and stronger, was that; the money was really spent on little more than the pleasures of eating, drinking, and the like. Now and then it is a joy to have one's table red with wine and roses, but you outstripped all taste and temperance. You demanded without grace and received without thanks. You grew to think that you had a sort of right to live at my expense and in a profuse luxury to which you had never been accustomed, and which for that reason made your appetites all the more keen, and at the end if you lost money gambling in some Algiers Casino you simply telegraphed next morning to me in London to lodge the amount of your losses to your account at your bank, and gave the matter no further thought of any kind.

When I tell you that between the autumn of 1892 and the date of my imprisonment I spent with you and on you more than £5000 in actual money, irrespective of the bills I incurred, you will have some idea of the sort of life on which you insisted. Do you think I exaggerate? My ordinary expenses with you for an ordinary day in London – for luncheon, dinner, supper, amusements, hansoms and the rest of it – ranged from £12 to £20, and the week's expenses were naturally in proportion and ranged from £80 to £130. For our three months at Goring my expenses (rent of course included) were £1340. Step by step with the Bankruptcy Receiver I had to go over every item of my life. It was horrible. *'Plain living and high thinking'* was, of course, an ideal you could not at that time have appreciated, but such extravagance was a disgrace to both of us. One of the most delightful dinners I remember ever having had is one Robbie and I had together in a little Soho café, which cost about as many shillings as my dinners to you used to cost pounds. Out of my dinner with Robbie came the first and best of all my dialogues. Idea, title, treatment, mode, everything was struck out at a 3 franc 50 c. table-d'hôte. Out of the reckless dinners with you nothing remains but the memory that too much was eaten and too much was drunk. And my yielding to your demands was bad for you. You know that now. It made you grasping often: at times not a little unscrupulous: ungracious always. There was on far too many occasions too little joy or privilege in being your host. You forgot – I will not say the formal courtesy of thanks, for formal courtesies will strain a close friendship but simply the grace of sweet companionship, the charm of pleasant conversation, that τερπνον κακον as the Greeks called it, and all those gentle humanities that make life lovely, and are an accompaniment to life as music might be, keeping things in tune and filling with melody the harsh or silent places. And though it may seem strange to you that one in the terrible position in which I am situated should find a difference between one disgrace and another, still I frankly admit that the folly of throwing away all this money on you, and letting you squander my fortune to your own hurt as well as to mine, gives to me and in my eyes a note of common profligacy to my Bankruptcy that makes me doubly ashamed of it. I was made for other things.

But most of all I blame myself for the entire ethical degradation I allowed you to bring on me. The basis of character is will-power, and my will-power became absolutely subject to yours. It sounds a grotesque thing to say, but it is none the less true. Those incessant scenes that seemed to be almost physically necessary to you, and in which your mind and body grew distorted and you became a thing as terrible to look at as to listen to: that dreadful mania you inherit from your father, the mania for writing revolting and loathsome letters: your entire lack of any control over your emotions as displayed in your long resentful moods of sullen silence, no less than in the sudden fits of almost epileptic rage: all these things in reference to which one of my letters to you, left by you lying about at the Savoy or some other hotel and so produced in Court by your father's Counsel, contained an entreaty not devoid of pathos, had you at that time been able to recognise pathos either in its elements or its expression: – these, I say, were the origin and causes of my fatal yielding to you in your daily increasing demands. You wore one out. It was the triumph of the smaller over the bigger nature. It was the case of that tyranny of the weak over the strong which somewhere in one of my plays I describe as being 'the only tyranny that lasts'.

And it was inevitable. In every relation of life with others one has to find some *moyen de vivre*. In your case, one had either to give up to you or to give you up. There was no other alternative. Through deep if misplaced affection for you: through great pity for your defects of temper and temperament: through my own proverbial good-nature and Celtic laziness: through an artistic aversion to coarse scenes and ugly words: through that incapacity to bear resentment of any kind which at that time characterised me: through my dislike of seeing life made bitter and uncomely by what to me, with my eyes really fixed on other things, seemed to be mere trifles too petty for more than a moment's thought or interest – through these reasons, simple as they

101

may sound, I gave up to you always. As a natural result, your claims, your efforts at domination, your exactions grew more and more unreasonable. Your meanest motive, your lowest appetite, your most common passion, became to you laws by which the lives of others were to be guided always, and to which, if necessary, they were to be without scruple sacrificed. Knowing that by making a scene you could always have your way, it was but natural that you should proceed, almost unconsciously I have no doubt, to every excess of vulgar violence. At the end you did not know to what goal you were hurrying, or with what aim in view. Having made your own of my genius, my will-power, and my fortune, you required, in the blindness of an inexhaustible greed, my entire existence. You took it. At the one supremely and tragically critical moment of all my life, just before my lamentable step of beginning my absurd action, on the one side there was your father attacking me with hideous cards left at my club, on the other side there was you attacking me with no less loathsome letters. The letter I received from you on the morning of the day I let you take me down to the Police Court to apply for the ridiculous warrant for your father's arrest was one of the worst you ever wrote, and for the most shameful reason. Between you both I lost my head. My judgment forsook me. Terror took its place. I saw no possible escape, I may say frankly, from either of you. Blindly I staggered as an ox into the shambles. I had made a gigantic psychological error. I had always thought that my giving up to you in small things meant nothing: that when a great moment arrived I could reassert my will-power in its natural superiority. It was not so. At the great moment my will-power completely failed me. In life there is really no small or great thing. All things are of equal value and of equal size. My habit – due to indifference chiefly at first – of giving up to you in everything had become insensibly a real part of my nature. Without my knowing it, it had stereotyped my temperament to one permanent and fatal mood. That is why, in the subtle epilogue to the first edition of his essays, Pater says that 'Failure is to form habits'. When he said it the dull Oxford people thought the phrase a mere wilful inversion of the somewhat wearisome text of Aristotelian Ethics, but there is a wonderful, a terrible truth hidden in it. I had allowed you to sap my strength of character, and to me the formation of a habit had proved to be not Failure merely but Ruin. Ethically you had been even still more destructive to me than you had been artistically.

As regards your letter to me in answer to this, it may be as long or as short as you choose. Address the envelope to 'The Governor, H.M. Prison, Reading'. Inside, in another, and an open envelope, place your own letter to me: if your paper is very thin do not write on both sides, as it makes it hard for others to read. I have written to you with perfect freedom. You can write to me with the same. What I must know from you is why you have never made any attempt to write to me, since the August of the year before last, more especially after, in the May of last year, eleven months ago now, you knew, and admitted to others that you knew, how you made me suffer, and how I realised it. I waited month after month to hear from you. Even if I had not been waiting but had shut the doors against you, you should have remembered that no one can possibly shut the doors against Love for ever. The unjust judge in the Gospels rises up at length to give a just decision because Justice comes knocking daily at his door; and at night-time the friend, in whose heart there is no real friendship, yields at length to his friend 'because of his importunity'. There is no prison in any world into which Love cannot force an entrance. If you did not understand that, you did not understand anything about Love at all. Then, let me know all about your article on me for the *Mercure de France*. I know something of it. You had better quote from it. It is set up in type. Also, let me know the exact terms of your Dedication of your poems. If it is in prose, quote the prose; if in verse, quote the verse. I have no doubt that there will be beauty in it. Write to me with full frankness about yourself: about your life: your friends: your occupations: your books. Tell me about your volume and its reception. Whatever you have to say for yourself, say it without fear. Don't write what you don't mean: that is all. If anything in your letter is false or counterfeit I shall detect it by the ring at once.

It is not for nothing, or to no purpose, that in my lifelong cult of literature I have made myself

> Miser of sound and syllable, no less
> Than Midas of his coinage.

Remember also that I have yet to know you. Perhaps we have yet to know each other.

For yourself, I have but this last thing to say. Do not be afraid of the past. If people tell you that it is irrevocable, do not believe them. The past, the present and the future are but one moment in the sight of God, in whose sight we should try to live. Time and space, succession and extension, are merely accidental conditions of Thought. The Imagination can transcend them, and move in a free sphere of ideal existences. Things, also, are in their essence what we choose to make them. A thing *is*, according to the mode in which one looks at it. 'Where others', says Blake, 'see but the Dawn coming over the hill, I see the sons of God shouting for joy.' What seemed to the world and to myself my future I lost irretrievably when I let myself be taunted into taking the action against your father: had, I dare say, lost it really long before that. What lies before me is my past. I have got to make myself look on that with different eyes, to make the world look on it with different eyes, to make God look on it with different eyes. This I cannot do by ignoring it, or slighting it, or praising it, or denying it. It is only to be done fully by accepting it as an inevitable part of the evolution of my life and character: by bowing my head to everything that I have suffered. How far I am away from the true temper of soul, this letter in its changing, uncertain moods, its scorn and bitterness, its aspirations and its failure to realise those aspirations, shows you quite clearly. But do not forget in what a terrible school I am sitting at my task. And incomplete, imperfect, as I am, yet from me you may have still much to gain. You came to me to learn the Pleasure of Life and the Pleasure of Art. Perhaps I am chosen to teach you something much more wonderful, the meaning of Sorrow, and its beauty.

Your affectionate friend
Oscar Wilde

A.E. HOUSMAN
1859 – 1936

Alfred Edward Housman's adored mother died when he was twelve years old. At Oxford he fell in love with fellow Freshman Moses 'Mo' Jackson. It was not a sexually requited relationship, but they happily set up lodgings together in Bayswater, London. Jackson married and went to India. At this time Housman wrote to him: 'You are largely responsible for my writing poetry and you ought to take the consequences.'

In 1900 he fell for a twenty-three-year-old Venetian gondolier. Subsequently, Housman visited the man every year, and when he heard the man was ill, settled an annuity on him. On the man's death, his family pestered Housman for more cash; there was speculation that they were blackmailing him over his relationship with their relative.

In 1935, Housman wrote to Blakeney, a printer:

Trinity College, Cambridge
20th December, 1935

Dear Mr. Blakeney,

Many thanks for the specimen of your private printing. If Watson had gone on writing things like 'Wordsworth's grave', and some other things which he wrote when he was thirty, he would have been one of the first poets of the age. But he swallowed the praises of *The Spectator*, and wrote a lot which he ought to have known was quite second-rate; and when early in this century he made a fresh start, the merit of his writing, which was sometimes considerable, was that of epigram rather than of poetry.

Thanks for enquiring after my health. It is weak and declining, and I have already lived more than two years too long.

Yours very truly,
A.E. Housman

ROGER CASEMENT
1864 – 1916

Casement was brought up by his Ulster Protestant uncle, named Bannister. Casement became a diplomat in Africa, where he compiled two reports on the suffering of the African people in the Congo, and the Indians in Brazil. He was knighted in 1911. In 1914, on the outbreak of war, Casement went to Germany to arrange an arms deal for the Irish cause. He was politically very active and tried in vain to stop the Easter Uprising in 1916. On April 12, 1916, he sailed in a German submarine accompanying a shipload of arms bound for Ireland. The ship was captured by the British. Casement himself was captured two weeks later in Ireland, and tried for treason.

An Irish freedom fighter, John Devoy, writes to Laurence de Lacy about the frustrations of working alongside the obstinate and reckless Casement...

20th July 1916

Dear Friend,

I avail myself of the chance of our friend returning to S.F. to send you the letter by hand. Nothing is safe in the mails in this free country.

Our information as to what occurred at home, on the inside, was very meagre up to a couple of weeks ago, though we had enough to enable us to guess the truth pretty accurately. Now authentic accounts coming by hand show us that we guessed very accurately. One is a young lady from your country, 'Miss R.'. She was in the thick of it all, and saw Seán McD. the night before he was shot. She went to London first and got a permit there to come out. She was sent by the women. So far as the leaders are concerned they are all either dead, in prison or 'on their keeping', but there are twenty men ready for work now for one there was before the fight. The same thing is told us by everybody, including priests with knowledge of the whole country.

We got a long letter from Cork containing a lot of information from there. It was sad as concerned the losses of leaders, but buoyant and most helpful. It was written by a woman on behalf of the men.

Then came a man who had been in prison and was released. He is from Kilkenny, and had very accurate information about what occurred immediately before the fight. Two men from there had attended the meeting in Dublin on Easter Sunday, where, after the mix-up about the countermand, it was decided to fight...

The substance of it all is that the betrayal of the information about the shipload of arms by Wilson's men enabled the English to catch the vessel. There is no doubt at all about this. They got in the raid on von Igel's office a note of mine – the transcript of a message received *in cypher from Dublin and wirelessed to Berlin the day before – 17th April – a request not to land the arms 'before the night of Sunday 23rd'*. That was its meaning, but it used the words 'Goods'. It was at once given to the English and they sent out their boats and caught the ship. Then they sent troops to Tralee and reinforced Limerick.

That would not have spoiled the rising, because if they were in the field other shiploads would have been sent. *Casement did the rest.* He landed on Friday and sent a message to MacNeill to stop it; that it was hopeless, etc. MacNeill got it on Saturday and issued his countermand. He got one message up by Monteith, who, of course, was obeying orders, and sent another by a priest, for whom he sent after his arrest. MacNeill had only been told of the decision on Good Friday – which was a great mistake. He was at first shocked, but on hearing of the shipload of arms consented. Then the Limerick and Kerry men got word to him of the sinking of the ship, and that, with the request from Roger, decided him and he issued the fatal order and took care that it reached everybody. From our experience of a year of his utter impracticability – he had been assuring us, till we were sick, that 'there was no hope for the poor old woman' until the next war – we sent with the first note from home that we transmitted to Berlin a request that R. *be asked to remain there*, 'to take care of Irish interests'. We knew he would meddle in his honest, but visionary way to such an extent as to spoil things, but we did not dream that he would ruin everything as he has done. He took no notice whatever of decisions or instructions, but without quarrelling, pursued his own dreams. The last letter I got from him, written last December, said the only hope now of making a demonstration that would impress the world was to send the 'Brigade' to Egypt. To *impress the world by sending sixty men to a place where they could do nothing*. We had told him nearly a year before that we would not consent to this but he took no notice. He was obsessed with the idea that he was a wonderful leader and that nothing could be done without him. His letters always kept me awake on the night of the day I got them. Miss R. says he told Duffy that the Germans treated us shamefully and that he had hard work to get the few arms that were on that ship: that they were no good, etc. Well, they were good enough for the Russians to overrun East Prussia with and to drive the Austrians across the Carpathians and if our fellows had got them they'd be able to shoot a good many Englishmen with them. It is not true that the Germans treated us badly; they did everything we asked, but they were weary of his impracticable dreams and told us to deal directly with them here. He had no more to do with getting that shipload than the man in the moon. The request was made from Dublin and we transmitted it from *here*. They replied in nine days and the message was sent to Dublin by a girl who had brought out the request.

He told Duffy that he wanted to be landed in Galway, to go to Dublin and lay the situation before them – that is, to tell them that Germany was not sincere, etc., and then if they decided to fight that *he would go out and die with them*. Every note he struck was one of despair. And he told everything to every fellow who called on him. Christensen who 'saved' him, is one of the worst crooks I ever met and was in the pay of the English all along. He, Casement, was warned of that from Ireland and the first thing he did was to tell the fellow himself and to give him the name of the man who had warned him. Christensen was going over from here to testify against him – and incidently to give away all our secrets that he had got from Roger, *but we kept him here*.

I don't want you to tell any of this – I mean about Roger – to anyone except Father Yorke, but the rest you can use your judgment about.

If that countermand had not been issued they could have taken Dublin and the big force that was concentrated on Dublin would have had to be divided up. They would not have known where to send it for a while and a lot of soldiers would have joined.

Only 1,500 men fought in Dublin and they held up an army of 20,000 or 25,000 Britishers for a whole week. Only 800 turned out at first; the rest came later, but after Tuesday those who wanted could not get near them and were half crazy. Our fellows had only 103 killed and wounded. The English had 2,700.

The turnover of the people to our side, according to everybody, is astonishing, partly because of the splendid fight and partly because of the atrocities, which were very extensive. The Dublin priests are collecting evidence about them and will publish the record. The conversions to our side among the priests is the most remarkable thing of all.

We have sent a good sum of money for *our* work and it is already there. We expect to be in direct communication with a reorganised S.C., or a partly reorganised one, very soon.

Of course, a lot of the future will depend on the course of the war which is now going somewhat against us, but whatever comes, the old Ireland is gone.

The most encouraging thing of all is that there was not one informer. Hundreds of the men knew the date, but the Government was in the dark until the blow was struck. There is no doubt at all about this. Seán told the girls that he was astonished at the utter absence of anything but the results of their shadowing, in the testimony of the Dublin detectives. Not a word of inside information. And he said their testimony was stupid.

I have struck this off on the typewriter in a desperate hurry, without any regard to style or sequence, because if I don't do it this evening I can't do it at all, and I tore one of the pages in taking it out and had to paste it. Reidy had been laid up for the past six weeks from eating bad crabs and I have been in a frightful mess in consequence. I nearly broke down two or three times. I have had Peter Golden helping me for the past three days and I am easier now. But it was the hardest ordeal I ever put in because I had to go out to see the messengers and attend committee meetings so often and then resume work, not knowing 'where I was at'.

With the few facts I have given you in your mind you will understand the situation better.

Kind regards to Mrs De L. and to Father Yorke.

Yours truly,
John Devoy

The Adler Christiansen mentioned in Devoy's letter, was a lover of Casement's. Christiansen, who had a reputation for lying, was unpopular with Casement's other friends; he dressed gaudily, using cosmetics, and monopolised Casement.

Casement's diaries, in the hands of the British police, did not help his plight:

> 'Several boys at Funchal in Madeira – Agostinho, $4'
> 'Las Palmas – fair hair... around 17... enormous'
> 'London – dusky depredator, huge, 7 inches'
> '1910 Madeira – splendid testiminhos, no bush to speak of.
>   Soft as silk and big and full. 1. 0/–'
> 'Carlos Augusta Costa – 189 Rue dos Ferreiros, Funchal. Very fine
>   one, big long thick – wants awfully and likes very much. 7/6d'

The question of Casement's innocence or guilt of treason was submerged under a welter of moralistic publicity surrounding the diary entries, which hardened public and legal attitudes against him. His cousin Gertrude Bannister, who had worked tirelessly for his release, received this letter from Prime Minister Asquith:

10 Downing Street
Whitehall
2 August 1916

Dear Madam,

It is with sincere pain (and only in compliance with your request) that I inform you that, after very full consideration, the Cabinet today came to the conclusion that there were not sufficient grounds for a reprieve.

I need not assure you that I wish it had been possible for them to arrive at a different decision.

Yours very faithfully,
H.H. Asquith

I am returning the documents.

Roger Casement was hanged in 1916, and pardoned posthumously in 1920.

MARCEL PROUST
1871 – 1922

*One of France's greatest novelists, and one of the great innovators in the
history of world literature, Marcel Proust devoted many years to his
celebrated novel* A la recherche du temps perdu. *It was one of the earliest
novels to portray a homosexual character with such insight and sympathy. In
1912, Proust was actively seeking a sympathetic publisher as well as
canvassing his friends for advice.*

TO EUGENE FASQUELLE

102 boulevard Haussman
28 October 1912

Monsieur,

M. Calmette has given me the most gratifying news in telling me
that you are prepared to publish my book. It is such a pleasure to me to
have it appear under your auspices that I was almost afraid it would
be unrealisable, like everything one badly wants; allow me then to
begin by expressing my gratitude.

I should like to warn you very frankly in advance that the work in
question is what used to be called an indecent work, indeed much
more indecent than what is usually published. If I feel obliged to go
into explanations in this respect, it's because I am sending you only my
first volume, which apart from a few rare passages is very chaste, and I
don't want to deceive you as to the rest, nor do I want to risk, once the
first volume has appeared, your refusing to publish the last two (or the
last, since perhaps the whole of the second part will fit into one large
volume).

This second part is entirely written but since it's in exercise books
and not typed I am not sending it to you in advance; the manuscript
included with this letter forms the substance of one volume only. What
is highly shocking in the second part is, I need hardly tell you, not in
the least gratuitous, and the overall character of the work will testify to
its high moral purpose. In giving you the following few details so that
you know in advance everything that might prompt you to reconsider

your benevolent decision, I should like to enjoin you to secrecy on a subject that no one knows of and that people might dissuade me from dealing with if it 'transpired'.

One of my characters (who emerge in the book as people do in life, that is to say scarcely known at first and often discovered long afterwards to be the opposite of what was thought) makes only a fleeting appearance in the first part as the lover of one of my heroines. Towards the end of the first part (or the beginning of the second, if the manuscript I'm sending you exceeds the limits of one volume) this character makes the narrator's acquaintance, puts on a show of virility, of contempt for effeminate young men, etc. But in the second part this elderly gentleman of a noble family reveals himself as a pederast who will be portrayed in a comic light but, without any obscene language, will be seen 'picking up' a concierge and 'keeping' a pianist. I think this character – the virile pederast bearing a grudge against effeminate young men who sell him a pup by turning out to be indistinguishable from women, a 'misanthrope' from having suffered through men, just as some men are misogynists from having suffered through women – I think this character is something new (especially in the way he is treated which I can't explain to you in detail here), and it's for that reason that I beg you not to talk to anyone about him. Moreover the very different subjects against which he is contrasted, the framework of poetry in which his ridiculous old age is embedded and juxtaposed – all that relieves this part of the book from the invariably painful character of a specialised monograph. Nevertheless and although no detail is shocking (or if so is saved by humour, as when the concierge calls this white-haired duke 'you big baby') I won't deny that it isn't a very 'usual' subject, and I thought it more honest to tell you so; more prudent too, because you must see what my situation would be if after the first volume of a work which is certainly the last I shall write and in which I have tried to encompass the whole of my philosophy, to voice the whole of my 'music', you broke it in two like a shattered vase by ending its publication there...

Marcel Proust

10 or 11 June 1914

Dear friend,

Thank you so much for having had the kindness to write to me. I fear that all too little of what I wanted to say has found its way into my prose, and that that which alone seemed to me worth taking the trouble to write remains unexpressed.

It is too good of you to think of my worries and sorrows as well; alas, the cup has overflowed with the death of a young man whom I loved probably more than all my friends since it has made me so unhappy. Although he was of the most humble 'condition' and devoid of culture, I have letters from him which are those of a great writer. He had a delightful intelligence, though it wasn't at all for that reason that I loved him. It took me a long time to realise it, but in fact less long than it took him. I discovered in him those qualities that were so marvellously incompatible with everything he was – discovered them with amazement, though they added nothing to my affection for him: I simply took pleasure in making him aware of them. But he died before he fully realised what he was, before he even became it entirely. The whole thing is mixed up with such appalling circumstances that, shattered as I already was, I don't know how I can endure such grief.

Thank you also for your indulgence towards Monsieur de Charlus. I tried to portray a homosexual infatuated with virility because, without knowing it, he is a Woman. I don't in the least claim that he is the only type of homosexual. But he's an interesting type which, I believe, hasn't ever been described. Like all homosexuals, moreover, he is different from the rest of men, in some ways worse, in many ways infinitely better. Just as one may say: 'There is a certain connection between the nervous or arthritic condition of such and such a person and his gifts of sensibility etc.', I'm convinced that it's because of his homosexuality that Monsieur de Charlus understands so many things which are a closed book to his brother the Duc de Guermantes, that he is so much more subtle and sensitive. I've emphasised this right from the start. Unfortunately, the effort of objectivity I've made there as elsewhere will make this book particularly obnoxious. In the third volume, where Monsieur de Charlus (who merely makes an appearance in this one) plays a considerable rôle, the enemies of homosexuality will be revolted by the scenes I shall describe.

As for this particular volume (in which incidentally Monsieur de Charlus will appear elsewhere than in the passage you've read), I don't know whether I should go on calling it *Le Côté de Guermantes*. In Russian and English and old French novels they put Part One and Part Two, and nobody is surprised if a 'Part' begins at the end of the first volume or ends at the beginning of the third. But with different titles for each volume! In reality, the first part of *Le Côté de Guermantes* still takes place on Swann's way, and the first third of the third volume on the Guermantes way. Should I leave this title and explain the inexactness in a note, or find another title for the second volume?

As for my general title *A la recherche du temps perdu*, Monsieur Ghéon's explication of it has been really unfortunate for me, for ever since (and this shows incidentally the great influence he has) not a single critic, whether Dutch or Breton, has failed to serve up the same reproaches, in less good prose. Yet it seems to me that 'temps perdu' must mean 'passé' and since I announced my third volume under the title *Le Temps retrouvé*, it was pretty clear that I was moving towards something, that the whole thing wasn't an idle dilettantish evocation. Ought I to have announced from the beginning what I would only disclose at the end? I don't think so, any more than I think that it would have been artistically right to reveal straight away that if Swann allowed Monsieur de Charlus to go out with Odette, it was because Charlus had been in love with Swann since their schooldays, so the latter knew that he need not be jealous.

Dear friend, I so much enjoy chatting to you that I'm over-tiring myself; so I shall say good-bye and thank you again, with my most affectionate and admiring regards.

Marcel Proust

ANDRÉ GIDE
1869 – 1951

André Gide's position in the history of French literature is one that has been hailed by three generations of his fellow writers from Malraux, via Sartre and Camus to Roland Barthes. His novels inhabit a world of sophisticated psychological probing into character and motive. *His masterpieces include* L'Immoraliste, La Porte Etroite, La Symphonie Pastorale *and* Les Faux-Monnayeurs. *Here, he replies to Proust's uncertainties about* A la recherche du temps perdu:

TO MARCEL PROUST

Cuverville
near Criquetot l'Esneval
Seine-Inférieure
14 June 1914

My dear friend,

I deeply regret not having gone round to knock on your door without ceremony during my last visit to Paris, and I curse this extreme discretion of mine which constantly paralyses me and by which my whole life is crippled.

I realise that I would have met with a closed door and strict orders, but even if there was only one chance in a hundred that that door might have been opened to me for an instant... I ought to have tried! And now that I know you are sadder still because of this bereavement, I cannot help but reiterate: if you wish to see me, send for me. I am used to invalids; I myself was ill for a long time; I know how to speak softly; I know how to listen; indeed, I especially know how to listen. Why do you hold yourself aloof from my friendship and allow me to suffer from the feeling that it is useless?

M. de Charlus is an admirable creation, through which you will have contributed to the habitual confusion between the homosexual and the invert. For the nuances and distinctions you point out in your letter not be accepted. Charlus, who is only a particular individual, will be taken as a type, and will lend himself to generalisation. What I am saying is entirely to the credit of your portrait. (Did you ever know the remarkable 'Baron d'Oazans' – I've forgotten how to spell his name – who died five or six years ago, of whom Charlus reminds me at times?) 'He doesn't care a fig for his old grandmother, does he, eh, little rascal?' is wonderful.

Don't be too upset, and above all don't be too surprised, to see your efforts at objectivity so little understood (the article I've just read in *L'Effort libre* is particularly obtuse). What is happening to your books is what happened to *L'Immoraliste* and *La Porte étroite*, which all the critics chose to see as personal confessions – without exactly explaining moreover that the one didn't make the other impossible. I very much hope that your books and mine are tough enough and especially durable enough to withstand all these fallacious interpretations. And I hope you are convinced of this.

I am nonetheless a little fearful lest hostile critics mislead opinion for a long time to come on the subject of *Les Caves*, and I am forced to admit that the book does lend itself to the worst misunderstandings. If I felt that you were less ill and unhappy I might perhaps have asked you to enlighten the public with an article in *Le Figaro* – for I know the reputation you enjoy among certain discerning people whom I am particularly anxious to reach, and your earlier letters showed me how deeply and subtly you had understood my novel.

Yours
André Gide

In 1947 André Gide was awarded the Nobel prize for literature.

E.M. FORSTER
1879 – 1970

The novelist and critic E.M. Forster is best known for his novels A Room with a View, A Passage to India, Howards End *and, largely due to its cinematic transformation,* Maurice, *a posthumously published novel that attempts to analyse homosexual love within the straitjacket of a largely conservative social niveau. He spent many years of his youth travelling, and from the First World War until the early 1920s he spent some time in Greece – where he met the poet C. P. Cavafy, whose poetry celebrating the love between men made a great impact on him – and India where he was secretary and companion to the Maharajah of Dewas Senior, a period that drew from him some very touching letters, for he was clearly deeply affected by the devotion of his charges and the Indians he met.*

TO ALICE CLARA FORSTER

Hyderabad
20 December 1921

Dearest Mummy;

I returned to find your welcome letter, but will begin by my own news, which is all pleasant. I have had such a wonderful time. The Mount Everest explorers speak of visiting places where no white man has been seen before, but I have had the same experience without fatigue or expense at Gangavati. The remoteness and the extent of Indian life are both wonderful. I described our journey to Gangavati in a letter to Aunt Laura; our official tour ended there, and very happily for Masood, who had a great ovation not only from the officials but from the inhabitants. I thought it was mostly the motor, but no; when we left in a bullock cart, the same crowds accompanied us, and would have proceeded far into the mountains but for his exhortations. We started late, because owing to the rejoicings over the arrival of Education, the driver of the bullocks was drunk and could not be found. Our journey was to Vijayanagar, the great ruined city of which you have heard me speak. Ali Akbar and myself walked for several miles while Masood slumbered in the cart. It was a solid but very comfortable edifice, padded inside with good brown leather, and decorated outside with paintings of cupids and sphinxes in the Persian style and with Hindu smears of good luck. Over it was an awning, you

117

climbed in behind by a waggling leather step. One bullock was large and white and its horns were painted vermilion and studded with brass at the tip: the other was dark and wizen. Although the country was perfectly safe, it gave the feeling of Robbers at every turn, it was so wild and tropical, palms of every description sticking up at every angle among masses of rock, and swift canals, the remains of the old irrigation system, rushing by the side of the track. The crossing of the Tungabhadra took over an hour. It is the frontier between Hyderabad and British India, a great rocky stream in a gorge. No boats in our sense of the word, but immense bowls of wicker work, coated with leather and propelled by a savage with a paddle. We stepped a-board, or a-saucer, Masood's foot seemed to go straight through the basket into the water and I thought we should sink. But we got across, revolving slowly like the three wise men of Gotham, the bullock-cart followed in another saucer – an incredible spectacle – then came two more each towing a swimming bullock, then three more with servants and luggage. The bullocks, especially the white one with scarlet horns, were affronted at the experience, and stood gazing sadly at the stream they had crossed and refused to eat. After they had rested we went on to Vijayanagar.

This is a wonderful place – a Hindu Empire, wiped out very suddenly about 400 years ago by its Mohammedan neighbours, whom it had ill-treated. The area is a rocky wilderness like Rustall Common on a gigantic scale, or Dartmoor, and between the precipices and boulders, the palaces and temples are fitted in. There were broad streets, too, but these have become rice fields, except the street leading up to the Great Temple of Hampi, which is still in use, like the temple itself; broader than anything we have in London, and still lined with deserted houses and shops. On the one side the Tungabhadra, among stupendous scenery, on the left, a covey of Jain Temples, perched on a long slope of rock like birds, closing the vista, the Great Temple; behind jagged Peaks, supporting more shrines and reached by granite stairways. The architecture was often inferior and always ornate, but Mummy would have loved the situations, had she the legs or even the feet to reach them. Oh we were tired. The bullocks could go no further, and we three walked about 6 miles after our arrival, and the next day Ali Akbar and I walked quite 10, with a policeman, stolen from

Hyderabad, to carry our books and bananas. The most remarkable work is the Throne Platform a series of terraces carved with camels, elephants, dancing girls, &c, and at the top, with views in every direction, a level place where the king used to sit. The Hindus mess up most of their effects, and no doubt there was some ornate and fiddling canopy; but in its present desolation the Platform is wonderful. I may also mention a granite doorway, where the Kings of Vijayanagar were weighed against gold, and the colossal and hideous statue of the Man-Lion God, with goggle eyes and a seven-headed serpent above him. But you will have done enough sight seeing. There is a wonder inconveniently situated at some distance from these great distances – was itself once a temple. Squatting creatures looked down on us while we ate and in the verandah, where I slept, lay a statue of Vishnu just my own size, with his two wives massaging his legs.

The bullock-cart – also stolen – took us at night to the R[ailwa]y Sta., whence M. and A. A. went east to Hyderabad, and I west for one more day's sightseeing alone. Nussu is excellent – so good that I think he is a spy; there are many in Hyderabad and I know that some of the officials are puzzled by the length of my stay. However, I am very glad to benefit at the expense of the Secret Service Fund. If indeed it does supply servants to globe trotters at less than the market rate, so much the better. My experiences – after reaching civilisation – were uncomfortable, bad food and much dirt, and Nussu was as willing as Hassan and far more competent, buying 14 bananas for 4d and carrying my bed endlessly about at night at Guntakal Station, in the search of some place which should be free from pilgrims, mosquitoes, mangy dogs, and the smell of oil. The people at Hyderabad are Telugus – black and thick, but not unattractive; at Gangávati we were among Canarese, many of whom had a wild beauty; at Guntakal I hit a new and most unattractive race, the Madrassi. They shave the front half of their head and greasy locks float behind; or they reverse the idea of the tonsure i.e. shave all but the crown and in the middle of that, like a snake curled on a mat, lies a pig tail. They speak English in silken tones. Their bodies are weak and thin. Horrid Madrassis! Now the Bengalis, when one gets first hand accounts of them instead of the conventional gossip, seem to be nice – intellectual, imaginative, and manly. I wish I had seen something of them. Nussu and I returned on Sunday.

Masood had a cold, but the Hydari girls very kindly met me in a car. – That concludes a most delightful time. I have missed out much and described the rest dully; I'll end by something very dull: a Time Table, so that you may see at a glance what we did.

Dec. 8th   Hyderabad to Raichur (rail)
9th Raichur
10th to Lingsagur by car, which we took with us.
11th & 12th Lingsagur
13th to Gangávati by car, as described in letter to Aunt Laura
14th Gangávati
15th to Vijayanagar – car going back empty over 100 miles to
     Raichur, as roads gave out
16th to Ry. sta. – where we parted at night, I reaching Banni Koppa
     morning of 17th and walking to the lonely temple of Ittagi in the
     dawn; train to Guntakal
18th where I slept, and, travelling all day reached Hyderabad.

Politics here have unexpectedly turned to the worse. The boys at one of the schools never turned up the day the Prince landed. The schoolmaster – so like a subordinate – never reported it to Masood, hoping to hush it up, and now the Police have found it out and – so like the Police – want a list of the boys who didn't come. Next step – all the scholars in Hyderabad will probably refuse to attend when the Prince processes here. The arrests elsewhere in India have exasperated everybody so much. I am very sorry for the authorities – except for those who invited the Prince to come. Now that he has come, they simply don't know what to do. If they do nothing, as at Bombay, there are riots. If they arrest right and left, as at Allafiabad, the boycotting becomes more and more spontaneous, and the streets for seven miles are absolutely deserted by the inhabitants when the Prince passes. To the educated Indian, whatever his opinions, this ill-omened visit does seem an impertinence. You can't solve real complicated and ancient troubles by sending out a good-tempered boy; besides, this naïve slap-the-back method, though the very thing for our Colonies, scarcely goes down in the East. People talk about his safety – but not about what he is or says or does; all that is ignored. He is just a piece of luggage that must be carried about carefully. – As for Hyderabad, there won't be trouble, but the authorities were expecting enthusiasm and are agitated in consequence.

HAROLD NICOLSON
1886 – 1968

The diplomat Harold Nicolson married Vita Sackville-West in 1913 and they enjoyed a happy liaison, both taking lovers of the same sex: Vita most famously with Virginia Woolf (whose novel Orlando *is in many ways an extended love-letter to her), and with Violet Trefusis). They were remarkably frank to each other about these relationships as Harold's letters from the Embassy show...*

TO VITA SACKVILLE-WEST

British Delegation, Paris
15 September 1919

I had a very busy day yesterday – chiefly with Maurice Hankey. I got some things done – at least I think I have. I must say Lloyd George is a dynamic person. I wish I could have a long talk with him, but he is too busy – and I have to do it through Hankey.

I have got such a funny new friend – a dressmaker, with a large shop in the Rue Royale, a charming flat at the Rond Point (where I spent the whole of Saturday night – sleeping on the balcony) and about 10 mannequins of surpassing beauty. I am lunching at the shop today. My dressmaker is only 27 – and it is rather sporting to launch out into so elaborate an adventure at that age. Mar would like my new friend, I think – very attractive. Such a nice flat too. I think I shall stay there when and if I come back and not go to the Majestic. There is a spare room and I would pay for my board.

Teheran
7 September 1926

My last letter was written at Pelur. I sat there scribbling to my darling under the tent and with a blanket over my knee. I had just finished when I saw Gladwyn *[Jebb]* coming down the path with a rifle slung over his shoulder – gaunt and slightly bearded. I was so delighted to see him as I was getting rather bored with Patrick Hepburn. I do hope Ben isn't *too* good looking. Hepburn is really amazingly beautiful, but it gives him the self-consciousness of a professional beauty. Which is tiresome. He is not in the least b.s. *[homosexual]* but he has got so used to being made-up-to that he rather expects it. Gladwyn and I teased him dreadfully. We said he was like Mrs Langtry *[mistress of Edward VII]*. Apart from his looks he is a rather soft and colourless youth with a lack of vitality and a great many rectory corners in his mind. One has the impression of his having been a mother's darling, and he has a lot of undigested ideas about having to keep up one's position: 'Of course I like some of those clever people but it's a bad thing to see too much of them.' He is not exactly a fool – but a youth who is at moments coyly skittish. Thus he is beginning (oh so slightly) to get on my nerves, and I regret the time when he lay there as a beautiful corpse.

All these reflections are provoked by thinking how glad, that grey Scotch morning, I was to see Gladwyn. He makes Hepburn, poor boy, look merely a little (or rather a huge) fancy piece. He makes him look terribly bedint – which is odd in a descendant of Bothwell. Poor Patrick, I fear he is the 'charming boy' and will become less so each year. But the contrast between him and Gladwyn was very striking: Gladwyn so absolutely real: Patrick so beautiful and so second-hand. Oh I do hope Benzie won't be like that.

Mar will smile at all this and think it is merely because Patrick was so stand-offish and that Hadji was re-buffed. Not so. Don't like sleeping with Archdeacons' daughters and didn't want to in the least, the moment the Deanery began to obtrude with his retreating fever. But it shows one how bloody critical we all are, and how we really don't like people who have no personality inside. Poor Patrick!

RUPERT BROOKE
1887 – 1915

Educated at Rugby, where he started writing poetry, and at Cambridge, Brooke was 'adopted' as the personification of all that Britain stood for as the First World War started and the true horrors were not yet known. He was extraordinarily handsome and combined sensitivity with masculinity. As a result he was perhaps overpraised in his time and his reputation inevitably declined in the years following the war. He is generally considered to have been a poet of immense potential who was never allowed to fulfill that promise. He died in 1915 of blood poisoning in the Dardanelles. Though probably not gay, he was part of a set at Cambridge who certainly experimented with members of their own sex and Brooke clearly had few qualms about trying it himself, as he wrote to a Cambridge friend, James Strachey:

10 July 1912

How things shelve back! History takes you to January 1912 – Archaeology to the end of 1910 – Anthropology to, perhaps, the autumn of 1909. –

The autumn of 1909! We had hugged & kissed & strained, Denham & I, on and off for years – ever since that quiet evening I rubbed him, in the dark, speechlessly, in the smaller of the two small dorms. An abortive affair, as I told you. But in the summer holidays of 1906 and 1907 he had often taken me out to the hammock, after dinner, to lie entwined there. – He had vaguely hoped, I fancy, – But I lay always thinking Charlie *[Lascelles]*.

Denham was though, to my taste, attractive. So honestly and friendlily lascivious. Charm, not beauty, was his *forte*. He was not unlike Ka, in the allurement of vitality and of physical magic – oh, but Ka has beauty too. – He was lustful, immoral, affectionate, and delightful. As romance faded in me, I began, all unacknowledgedly, to cherish a hope – But I was never in the slightest degree in love with him.

In the early autumn of 1909, then, I was glad to get him to come and stay with me, at the Orchard. I came back late that Saturday night. Nothing was formulated in my mind. I found him asleep in front of the fire, at 1.45. I took him up to his bed, – he was very like a child when he was sleepy – and lay down on it. We hugged, and my fingers wandered a little. His skin was always very smooth. I had, I remember, a vast erection. He dropped off to sleep in my arms. I stole away to my own room: and lay in bed thinking– my head full of tiredness and my mouth of the taste of tea and whales [*sardines*], as usual. I decided, almost quite consciously, I *would* put the thing through next night. You see, I didn't at all know how he would take it. But I wanted to have some fun, and, still more, to see what it was *like*, and to do away with the shame (as I thought it was) of being a virgin. At length, I thought, I shall know something of all that James and Norton and Maynard and Lytton know and hold over me.

Of course, I *said* nothing.

Next evening, we talked long in front of the sitting room fire. My head was on his knees, after a bit. We discussed sodomy. He said he, finally, thought it *was* wrong... We got undressed there, as it was warm. Flesh is exciting, in firelight. You must remember that *openly* we were nothing to each other – less even than in 1906. About what one is with Bunny (who so resembles Denham). Oh, quite distant!

Again we went up to his room. He got into bed. I sat on it and talked. Then I lay on it. Then we put the light out and talked in the dark. I complained of the cold: and so got under the eiderdown. My brain was, I remember, almost all through, absolutely calm and indifferent, observing progress, and mapping out the next step. Of course, I had planned the general scheme beforehand.

I was still cold. He wasn't. 'Of course not, you're in bed!' 'Well then, you get right in, too'. – I made him ask me – oh! without difficulty! I got right in. Our arms were round each other. 'An adventure!' I kept thinking: and was horribly detached.

We stirred and pressed. The tides seemed to wax. At the right moment I, as planned, said 'come into my room, it's better there...' I suppose he knew what I meant. Anyhow he followed me. In that large bed it was cold; we clung together. Intentions became plain; but still nothing was said. I broke away a second, as the dance began, to slip my pyjamas. His was the woman's part throughout. I had to make him take his off – do it for him. Then it was purely body to body – my first, you know! I was still a little frightened of his, at any too sudden step, bolting; and he, I suppose, was shy. We kissed very little, as far as I can remember, face to face. And I only rarely handled his penis. Mine he touched once with his fingers; and that made me shiver so much that I think he was frightened. But with alternate stirrings, and still pressures, we mounted. My right hand got hold of the left half of his bottom, clutched it, and pressed his body into me. The smell of sweat began to be noticeable. At length we took to rolling to and fro over each other, in the excitement. Quite calm things, I remember, were passing through my brain. 'The Elizabethan joke "The Dance of the Sheets" has, then, something in it.' 'I hope his erection is all right' – and so on. I thought of him entirely in the third person. At length the waves grew more terrific: my control of the situation was over; I treated him with the utmost violence, to which he more quietly, but incessantly, responded. Half under him and half over, I came off. I *think* he came off at the same time, but of that I have never been sure. A silent moment: and then he slipped away to his room, carrying his pyjamas. We wished each other 'Goodnight'. It was between 4 and 5 in the morning. I lit a candle after he had gone. There was a dreadful mess on the bed. I wiped it as clear as I could, and left the place exposed in the air, to dry. I sat on the lower part of the bed, a blanket round me, and stared at the wall, and thought. I thought of innumerable things, that this was all; that the boasted jump from virginity to Knowledge seemed a very tiny affair, after all; that I hoped Denham, for whom I felt great tenderness, was sleeping. My thoughts went backward and forward. I unexcitedly reviewed my whole life, and indeed the whole universe. I was tired, and rather pleased with myself, and a little bleak. About six it was grayly daylight; I blew the candle out and slept till 8. At 8 Denham had to bicycle in to breakfast with Mr Benians, before catching his train. I bicycled with him, and turned off at the corner of – , is it Grange Road? –. We said scarcely anything to each other. I felt sad at the thought he was perhaps hurt and angry, and wouldn't ever want to see me again. – He did, of course, and was exactly as ever. Only we never referred to it. But that night I looked with some awe at the room – fifty yards away to the West from the bed I'm writing in – in which I Began; in which I 'copulated with' Denham; and I felt a curious private tie with Denham himself. So you'll understand it was – not with a *shock*, for I'm far too dead for that, but with a sort of dreary wonder and dizzy discomfort – that I heard Mr Benians inform me, after we'd greeted, that Denham died at one o'clock on Wednesday morning, – just twenty four hours ago now.

125

T.E. LAWRENCE
(Lawrence of Arabia)
1888 – 1935

Thomas Edward Lawrence, the explorer and scholar, joined the archaeologist Hogarth on an expedition to Jerablus on the Euphrates, to excavate the site of Carchemish. Lawrence was only eighteen. On the site, he met Sheikh Ahmed, nicknamed Dahoum (which means 'darkness' – he was very pale). Lawrence taught the boy to read and take photographs, and found in him a kindred spirit who shared dangers and hardships with him. Dahoum became his most intimate Arab friend.

In this letter, Lawrence writes to his twelve-year-old brother (there were five brothers including Thomas) from the dig. He signs the letter 'N' – short for 'Ned':

July 21, 1912

Ancient beast, It is about a year since we wrote letters to one another: suppose we do it again? It doesn't cost anything but time, and of time, do you know, I have mints just now. This is the first time for years and years that I have been able to sit down and think, and it is so precious a discovery: and one that so many people want to take from you.

Just now I am in Jerablus, and feeling matronly. Also I am house-physician, for you never saw such an establishment as mine has been this week. There are seven of us here – six Wahids and myself. First of all I had malaria – a short spell of the usual two-day sort. Mrs Haj Wahid got a new baby, and turned very ill.

Haj's boy fell down and broke his head to pieces and had to be tied up; Haj himself went drinking and collapsed with internal troubles of sorts. So I brought in Dahoum to help Haj's mother in the kitchen, and he ungratefully produced malignant malaria (autumno-æstival) and raved his head off for three days until he nearly died. I had to sit on his chest half one night to keep him in bed. The little Armenian doctor did the main part of the work (he's our consulting physician) and now Haj and Dahoum are convalescent, and more trouble than ever. This morning, when I woke up, Dahoum (who can just stand) was trying to sweep out the big room with the [help of keeping] hold-fasts of the tables and chairs, and Haj Wahid was feeding his donkey. I have to watch them all day to keep them in bed. Mrs Wahid has to go to Aleppo for an operation, much to the disgust of Haj. I had a mighty battle with him to get consent, for operation is anathema in the eyes of the doctors of his religion, and he wanted to save the money for a new one. He is angry because he has two daughters now.

Nice people these… they think Father the most miraculously fortunate man – in fact they suspect him of female infanticide. In a few days therefore I am to be alone in Jerablus, for all the others (but Dahoum) will be in Aleppo. Nice place Aleppo, warm, though too hot just now, and there is scarcity of water, for the crocodiles. They line all the canals you know, and swallow the water as it comes down from the river: everything in Aleppo loves water. Even the hippopotami sit all day on the kerb with their feet cooling in the gutters, and when sunset comes they boom for very joy, till all the valley is giddy with the sound. We have nothing like that here in Jerablus, which is a country place without hippopotami: but we have frogs who croak in chorus old, old tunes that Aristophanes taught them, and iguanas who sup in kings' sepulchres. And talking of sepulchres I bought such a lovely one last week: a crematory urn, a glazed jug of Babylonian work, some Hittite terracotta horses, and bronze fibulae: one of our first finds.

I have turned school-master, O tumult, and taught up to 11 times table a class whose average age was about seventeen. Then the house became a hospital, and I put an end to the local education authority. It was sad for they did so want to learn twelve times. It was a very wonderful school: everybody who got a table right got a lump of sugar each time. We finished two large tins! I took a class of four (including our Commissaire) in local history (special subject) and had the mollah of the district to listen to my lecture on geography. They can't make out why, if the world is really round, the people on the other side don't fall off. All this is stopped now and the head-master is reduced to writing nonsense to a worm...

Have just been interrupted by a spider as big as a whale's nebula: bottled him in whiskey for you: such hooked teeth and toes: I took him for a crab when he knocked at the door and said 'come in'. Such a fright: Salaams to the world.

N.

When the First World War broke out, T.E. Lawrence was attached to the intelligence section in Egypt. He loved the Arabs, and traditional Arab culture, and worked hard to free Syria from the Turks. The following extraordinary despatch is more lyrical than the form usually allows for, and betrays Lawrence's passion for the desert:

January 8th, 1917

On January 2, 1917, I left Yambo and rode across the plain to the mouth of Wadi Agida in five hours. From the mouth of Wadi Agida to the watershed into the Wadi Yambo basin was one hour, and thence to Nakhl Mubarak was one hour; all done at a four miles an hour walk. The lowest third of the ascent of Wadi Agida was over sand: soft, slow going. The upper parts were harder and better: the divide was slow and easy, and it gave at once to the eastward, on to a broad open valley, coming from the left with only very low hills on each side (Jebel Agida?), down which the road curved gently into Nahkhl Mubarak. The 'Sebil' stands about 400 yards east of the watershed.

The road down to Nakhl looked very beautiful today. The rains have brought up a thin growth of grass in all the hollows and flat places. The blades, of a very tender green, shoot up between all the stones, so that looked at from a little height and distance there is a lively mist of pale green here and there over the surfaces of the slate-blue and brown-red rocks. In places the growth was quite strong, and the camels of the army are grazing on it.

In Nakhl Mubarak I found Feisal encamped in tents: he himself was in his private tent, getting ready to go out to his reception. I stayed with him that day, while rumours came in that the Turkish force had evacuated Wadi Safra. One reported that from Bir Sheriufi to Bir Derwish was one great camp, and that its units were proceeding to Medina; another had seen a great force of camelmen and infantry ride East past Kheif yesterday. We decided to send out a feeler towards Hamra, to get news.

On January 3, I took thirty-five Mahamid and rode over a dull tamarisk-and thorn-grown plain past Bir Faqir (not seen) to Bir Wasit, which is the old Abu Khalaat of my first trip. We waited there till sunset, and then went to Bir Murra, left our camels with ten of the men, and the rest of us climbed up the hills north of the Haj road up to Jebel Dhifran, which was painful, for the hills are all of knife-like strata which are turned on edge, and often run in straight lines from crest to valley. It gives you abundance of broken surface but no sound grips, as the strata are so minutely cracked that almost any segment will come away from its socket in your hand.

The top of Dhifran was cold and misty. At dawn we disposed ourselves in crevices of the rocks, and at last saw three bell tents beneath us to the right, behind a spur at the head of the pass, 300 yards away. We could not get round to them to get a low view, so put a few bullets through their top. This turned out a crowd of Turks from all directions. They leaped into trenches and rifle pits each side of the road, and potting them was very difficult. I think they suffered some loss, but I could not be sure. They fired in every direction except towards us, and the row in the narrow valley was so awful that I expected to see the Hamra force turn out. As the Turks were already ten to our one this might have made our getting away difficult, so we crawled back and rushed down into a valley, almost on top of two very scared Turks, who may have been outposts or may have been at their private morning duty. They were the most ragged men I have ever seen, bar a British tramp, and surrendered at once...

At Nakhl Mubarak I found letters from Captain Warren saying that Zeid was still in Yambo, and the *Dufferin* would wait in Sherm Yambo till I came. As Feisal was just starting for Owais, I changed my camel

129

and rode down with him and the army to the head of Wadi Messarid by 3pm. The order of march was rather splendid and barbaric. Feisal in front, in white: Sharaf on his right in red headcloth and henna dyed tunic and cloak; myself on his left in white and red; behind us three banners of purple silk, with gold spikes; behind them three drummers playing a march, and behind them again, a wild bouncing mass of 1,200 camels of the bodyguard, all packed as closely as they could move, the men in every variety of coloured clothes, and the camels nearly as brilliant in their trappings, and the whole crowd singing at the tops of their voices a warsong in honour of Feisal and his family. It looked like a river of camels, for we filled up the Wadi to the tops of its banks, and poured along in a quarter of a mile long stream.

At the mouth of Wadi Messarid I said goodbye to Feisal and raced down the open plain to Yambo by 6pm. I was riding Feisal's own splendid camel, and so managed to do the twenty-two miles fairly easily. To my great relief I found the *Dufferin* had already left for Rabugh with Zeid, and so I was saved a further ten miles' march to Sherm Yambo.

JEAN COCTEAU
1889 – 1963

A genuine polymath, Jean Cocteau was a novelist, poet, playwright, film maker, designer and aesthetic activist. He received early encouragement from Sergei Diaghilev, the impresario who created the celebrated Ballets Russes and whose famous command, 'Astonish me', was guaranteed to instil in the young Cocteau a hunger for originality, a quality he was short of. Among his many collaborators were a group of young composers who went under the name, Les Six; one of whom was Francis Poulenc. Together they created Les mariés de la tour Eiffel, Le gendarme incompris, Le train bleu *and* La voix humaine *(the design of which he discusses below). The singer who was to create the rôle of the heroine, 'Elle', distraite at the end of a telephone, was Denise Duval.*

TO FRANCIS POULENC

Santo-Sospir,
St Jean Cap-Ferrat
6 December 1958

Mon très cher Francis, Take this letter to our Karuska ladies as they understand me even before I have uttered a word. Voilà:

The appearance of the character must not be tragic. It must not be frivolous.

No studied elegance.

The young woman has simply put on what was to hand but she is waiting for that telephone call from her lover *and believes she will be visible* to him.

In spite of her lie about the pink dress, there is a natural elegance about her, that of a young woman used to looking elegant.

The tragic touch will come from a shawl, or a trench-coat, or a loden, which she will throw over her shoulders without a trace of coquetterie because she is cold, 'cold within'. This is how I will show her inner coldness on stage.

Attached is a drawing of the costume.

I embrace you.

Jean

If Duval likes, she can put a ribbon in her hair, but I don't favour it.

The hairstyle – as Duval usually wears it but as if she had not been to the hairdresser for a long time.

No jewellery. The tunic must be in a shiny cloth. As we want to avoid black, it will have to be in the same, dark, blood-red of the curtains. (Phone Lavardet.) At Karuska's they know those oriental tunics with little high collars and slits in the sleeves. She has put this on over a white nightdress – long, puffed sleeves gathered in at the wrist – quite crumpled and very long, right down to her feet, which are in little red mules. (Nothing left bare.)

For the hairstyle, will you ask Duval to go with you to Alexandre's, in the rue du Faubourg St-Honoré. Tell him I sent you and explain the position to him. By far the best idea for the theatre is a small wig so that the disorder is deliberate – and is there once and for all. Alexandre is the only one who knows how to create this pastiche.

Tell Duval that all women resist the notion of a wig and then come running to him in a panic, *too late*, at the last minute. This is how he saved Marie Bell and the Offenbach actresses. Nothing is as ugly as a woman with her hair in a mess! But the effect is quite the opposite if enhanced by one of Alexandre's minuscule wigs.

Tell Alexandre that I want hair that is slightly reddish, or with red tints in it, through which she has run her hands a thousand times during the last few days.

It is essential to highlight the forehead and to leave it completely bare.

VASLAV NIJINSKY
1889–1950

The ballet dancer Vaslav Nijinsky was the son of dancers and brought up in the tradition. After appearing at the Maryinsky Theatre he became the star of the impresario Sergei Diaghilev's company for whom he created many of the most celebrated rôles of the early years of this century, including Petrushka, L'après-midi d'un faune *and* Le Sacre du Printemps. *His appearances in* Giselle *at the Maryinsky caused a scandal because his costume was considered indecent. He was Diaghilev's lover for a number of years but while on tour in South America he married Romola de Pulszky, a Hungarian dancer. Diaghilev severed all connection with the young man and his career began to wane. He danced for the last time in 1919 and for the rest of his life suffered increasingly from dementia praecox. He died in London.*

TO SERGEI PAVLOVICH DIAGHILEV

I cannot name you because I have no name for you. I am not writing to you hastily. I don't want you to think that I am nervous, I am not. I am able to write quite calmly. And I like to do it, although I am not expressing myself in beautiful sentences. I have never studied how to do this. And what I want is to express a thought.

I am not afraid of you, I know well that in your innermost being you do not hate me. I love you as one loves a human being, but I do not want to work with you. But there is one thing I want you to know, that I am working a great deal. I am not dead. I am still alive. God lives in me and I live in Him. My whole time is taken up with my dancing, and my work is progressing. Whenever I can I write, too, but not beautiful sentences, which you like so much.

You are organising troupes, I am not. I am not interested in forming companies – I am interested in Human beings.

You are dead because your aims are death.

I do not call you my friend, knowing that you are my bitter enemy, but even so I have no ill feelings towards you. Enmity calls for death and I am longing for life... You are malicious. I have deep sympathy and understanding for mankind. So had Dostoievsky. He was a kind man.

You said that I am a fool and I thought that you are one. I don't want to humiliate myself before you and you love people who do that. I do not want your smile, it is death... I do not smile any more, I don't bring destruction. I am not writing in order to make you merry, I am writing to make you cry.

I am a person with feeling and brains. You have brains but no feeling. Your sentiments are pernicious. You want to annihilate me and I want to save you. I love you but you don't love me. I wish you everything good, you wish me everything bad.

I know all your tricks. In the past when I was with you I often pretended to be nervous, but I was not an urchin. I was thinking deeper. I had God near me but you are a beast and do not understand love.

Don't think, don't hearken. I am not yours, you are not mine. I love you now, I loved you always. I am yours and I am my own. You have forgotten what God is, and so had I, in the past. But I found Him. You are the one who wants death and destruction, although you are afraid of death. I am not afraid of it. Death is a necessary event. We all have to die, therefore I am always prepared for it. I love love, but I am not the flesh and blood, I am the spirit, the soul. I am love... You did not want to understand me to live with me in true friendship. I wish you everything good.

I want to explain to you a great deal, but I never again want to work with you, as you have utterly different aims. You are a hypocrite, and I don't want to become one. I can only admire hypocrisy when a man wants to achieve something good and noble through this means.

You are a bad man, you are not a Tsar, a ruler. You are not my Emperor. You are an evil person. You wish me harm, but I do not want this for you. I am a tender being and want to write you a cradle song... a lullaby.

Sleep peacefully, sleep, sleep peacefully.
Man to Man
Vaslav Nijinsky

J. R. ACKERLEY
1896 – 1967

Joe Randolph Ackerley was one of England's greatest literary editors. He ran the art and book pages of The Listener *from 1935 until 1959. During those years he engaged some of the most distinguished writers and treated all with a respect and honesty that remain legendary; he was also a poet, playwright and novelist. His entire life is characterised by a loathing of censorship or anything repressive. His devotion to his Alsatian bitch, Queenie – the one creature whose feelings he never had to doubt – is a deeply moving episode in his life, one which inspired the book* My Dog Tulip *and which underlies his novel,* We Think the World of You. *At the age of 32 he learned that his father had another family, a startling discovery which prompted the posthumously published memoir* My Father and Myself.

TO FRANCIS KING

Athens
21 June 1960

Dearest Francis

I am flying out of Athens tomorrow, returning to Marseille and Provence, thence home. Another letter before I go. I've enjoyed myself here, though in a baffled and frustrated way: my true misfortune was that you are not here. I left notes on Brian de Jongh and Peter Sheldon; the latter never answered though I believe he is here; the former phoned and, after a lot of Greek muddles – the Palladion Hotel where I was staying had my name down wrong – contacted me and took me to dine on the Plaka. He took a lot of trouble over me, but alas I saw him only that once – and at that once we were not alone, E. Gathorne-Hardy and an adenoidal dull young American (name forgotten) were in the party. I asked de Jongh back, and fixed it, but further muddles occurred, English this time, he had to cancel and I never saw him more. As you say, he is a nice man and I would have welcomed a little private conversation with him. For I was there alone, my own American friends had gone off to Mykonos; moreover, Gathorne-Hardy disappeared into Samos, Peter Mayne, who was here, vanished somewhere, and although Henry Reed suddenly materialised later from England and kept me a couple of days company, he knew no more of Athens than I did.

[—] both saved and destroyed my life – at least I think so. I had just begun an affair with a boy of 16, and [—] told me that there was a law against tampering with the under-aged. Of this, I had no inkling, and the news unnerved me. The hotel had regarded the boy, when I had taken him in that day, with what I thought too deep an interest; nevertheless I had got him to my room and we had both had an enjoyable time for a couple of hours. He was a street boy (from Piraeus) – as with Lolita, he did the picking-up, one of a group of naughty boys who operate round the Rex cinema in Venizelos; but he had a nice, affectionate nature, was gay, considerate, active, not grasping and exceedingly prettily made, and, by the sun, coloured. I meant to keep on with him throughout my stay, and had a date with him for the next day – but [—]'s remark unnerved me. [—] had also said: 'Don't enter with the boy' – but I had: since I could speak no Greek, he no English, it would have been hard to concoct any other plan, my phrase-book does not help.

I should now provide an elaborate description of the set-up of the Palladion Hotel, which is, as perhaps you remember, on Venizelos, down by Omonia. Enough to say that sometimes, too rarely, at the reception desk a girl or two functioned: sometimes the manager and an older more authoritative sort of man whom I took to be the proprietor were added. In fact, usually there seemed far too many people about, to welcome one and get one into the lift. I must add that everyone was, and continued to be, extremely friendly to me – most attentive – and the 'proprietor' kept saying that he hoped I found staying there 'just like home' – in spite of my rejoinder (which I don't suppose he understood) that it was from 'home' that I was attempting to escape. At any rate, so far as I recall, when I slipped in with my boy, only the two women were functioning.

Anyway, I was unnerved; I did not keep my appointment with the boy the next day, though he did, I saw him from across the road, smartly dressed in a provocative way, arsing about with the other boys who haunted the 'Rex'. Sorry though I was, I decided to avoid him in future. (I saw him some days later, very gay and naughty, no heart-break!)

Four days later, as Henry Reed and I were returning from lunch at Vassily's (Henry was in the Alpha Hotel), another boy offered himself, also very pretty. He too could speak no English, but managed to convey that he was a Turkish tourist from Ankara – a story which I have subsequent reason to disbelieve. He was a little older than boy No. 1, either 17 or 18, smartly dressed in a cheap way. Henry soon made himself scarce, I conveyed to the boy that I lived in a hotel down the road, he said he would like to go in with me, and in we went. A bad moment? Everyone was in the foyer, proprietor, manager, two female receptionists, and two of the positively hideous pages the hotel seemed to have thought it wiser to select. Much polite fussification, 'how do you do?' to me, lift pressed for me, nervous conversation from me, everyone most civil, the manager himself rode us up to my floor, more nervous conversation from me. The boy and I entered my room. My dear, we had not been there two minutes before the phone rang. I picked it up – muffled, muddled voices, excited tones – then it emerged that it was a call for the boy in my room. Perplexedly, I handed the phone to him. More excited conversation – of which I understood not a word, but certainly heated, the sort of 'so what!' tone, then he put the receiver down, said 'The Police!' in an agitated way, added 'give me 3 drachmas', I gave 5, he grabbed his little hold-all, and positively fled.

What was it all about? What did he want 3 drachmas for? Who on earth had known he was in my room? Would he return? Well, I could write a lot more about it – speculation etc. – but I won't. He didn't return. I questioned the manager, very friendly, no change. 'Someone phoned saying he had seen a young boy enter the hotel in company with an Englishman. He wished to speak to the boy. Of course, I had to put him through!'

Well, there seem to me three possibilities only: (the boy himself must have been innocent, for he reaped nothing from it but 5 drach-mas); (i) a jealous discarded friend of the boy's had seen our pick-up and dished us, (ii) the police had seen us, and dished us, (iii) the proprietor himself, pretending to be a policeman, had dished us. I think the first rather fanciful and reject it. Which of the other two was right I haven't a clue, but it didn't matter, they had the same effect – I simply couldn't, afterwards, take anyone else into the hotel at all. Whoever was watching me, I was a watched, or at least noticed man, either the proprietor had discreetly informed [on] me (he was as nice as pie afterwards) that he wasn't going to have things like that in his hotel, or the police had seen and phoned (scouting round afterwards I observed that the kiosk exactly opposite the entrance to the hotel had a phone). So although I have felt as sexy as the devil I have simply had to give everything up since: I incline to adolescents, as you know, and they incline towards me. But I don't think I would dare to take even an adult in – a sailor, for example. So my Athens life has been ruined. And how I have wished you were here! I've thought of changing my hotel – but to what? [—] told me he lived in a louche hotel – a sort of brothel – wonderfully cheap, on the Plaka, and I think I found it in his absence. I have visited a dozen hotels observing the set-up, managerial faces, asking for prices, but I didn't move. I have only two or three more days here anyway – and how, after all, should I know whether a hotel that admitted whatever he liked without bother (does he like the brutal?) would also admit what I like, the very young, against the law, without bother? And it is so terribly hot, one really does want a shower in one's room: so does one's boy, and how nice it is to see him taking a shower. Perhaps I should have moved to the Grande Bretagne where, I am told, anything may happen, and indeed it is the middling, family hotel, like the Palladion, which is the difficulty. One wants one so poor and tiny that there are no public rooms for entertaining friends, or one with public rooms so many and so vast that no one can keep track of one's activities.

Dearest Francis, perhaps next year, or the next, you and I could rent an apartment in Athens for the spring. How delicious that would be. I do think the Athenians most attractive and wonderfully endowed. Last time I came I was not in the humour, not awake, I am wide awake now.

Anyway (i) how could I get away from [—], who was determined not to get away from me? and (ii) too much time was spent among tattered English and American queens in Zonar's and in those tiresome tavernas (not visited at all this trip) which cater only for those who like he-men and Tarzans! I don't think you ever took me to a Secondary or even Public School or Borstal. My tastes, I now realise, lie in that direction.

Best love

Joe

P.S. I am glad to go, yet sorry. I have missed a lot, I know, so much is going on. Yet how hard it is to get on without a common language (not just love itself, there I don't at all mind not being able to communicate a thought, but in the arranging, situating and defending of love) . Besides getting oneself into trouble, it would be terrible to involve young boys in one's follies – ready though they do seem to be involved. [–] says there is an animus against the whole thing. I have no means of knowing, and don't want to end up in a Greek gaol (better than English – gayer, I mean – though they may well be) or to land nice little boys there either.

But, I have a second string, with details of which I will not burden an already over-long letter. If he materialises, my lonely week here will be improved though not an intelligible word shall we be able to exchange.

Dear Francis, you cannot write to me here, but you can write to me in Putney. To come out in the autumn to you will mean ordinary London suits I suppose. Plus an overcoat.

Best love

Joe

E.M. Forster was another of Ackerley's regular correspondents. Their friendship dated back to 1922 (Ackerley was 26, Forster 43) and continued until the elder man's death in 1970. It was a relationship that was of immense importance to Ackerley, particularly when they discovered they were, albeit distantly, related. In 1960 he wrote from the YMCA in Tokyo with news of his exploits:

139

TO E.M. FORSTER

Y.M.C.A, Tokyo
8 November 1960

Dearest Morgan

I have not written to you for some time. As soon as I got to Tokyo, in a deluge of rain a week ago I began to feel perfectly happy here in Japan, really for the first time. I don't know why, perhaps not being with Europeans but on my own for a change: unfair to Jim, who is a dear. The Y.M.C.A. is a splendid hostel, hideously ugly outside, like a railway station within. But comfortable and cheap (14/- a night compared with the 38/- I paid here in a 'cheap' hotel I was stuffed in when I first came) and a constant *va et vient* of people of all nationality, but mostly Japanese and mostly young. It was my birthday two days later and I was given the nicest present in the world. At 9.30 p.m. The time mattered because it brought it all about. I was sitting in my bedroom concocting an article for *The Listener* (they've asked me) – Impressions of Japan – and you may be surprised to hear, – giving it and the Japanese the highest praise – , when I found my watch had stopped. There was a clock in the passage near the communal wash-house and I went to look. And a young man came out of the wash-house at that moment and gave me a backward look as he went to his room. The whole thing came out of the blue and took place in a trice. He left his door ajar for me to follow. He is a Japanese. His name is Saito. Since then he has been to my room. Once again from the wash-house (one has to wait and hang about, anything but embarrass) 'I will come to your room in a few minutes.' He was going to have a bath after his day's work. He is a businessman, somewhere between 25 and 30, a salesman in a brewery (how romantic!), to me very beautiful. He came in fresh and spotless linen, smelling of scent. So affectionate. So kind. He has been in America for a bit and can speak English. Of course I knew it would happen. The question was where. I thought it might happen in Sendai, but it didn't. It is a country where it must happen; age does not matter and the Japanese are so charming and uninhibited and curious, and so affectionate. It has made a great difference to my outlook – everything is all right now, I know – and so the question is whether and when I go to Kyoto. I like Francis, he is kind too, but I don't think I can bear the Europeans and Americans any longer. They put a rubbishy note on everything. They are here too, I go out with them from time to time – round the bars and the cinemas (the 'feelies', you get 'felt' as you stand in the back of the crowd). It is all 'cute little numbers' and the size of things. They seem not interested in anything but constant change. It is so dull and so expensive. I am pleased with my Saito, and grateful to him. I am all right with him, I know. I don't want to go to Francis – I don't want to come back to England – there is nothing for me there in Putney – excepting my darling Queenie. I do think of her. She has been so very sweet to me. But Nancy – yes I think of her too – would be so upset if I left her too long. I see all that. But for me, excepting to watch my dog die, there is nothing at all. I must decide whether to stay on here near Saito, if it works out all right (I think it will) or make a change. I am tired of changes, and there will be nothing for me in Kyoto except temples, the slaves of Osaka and the cheapness of staying in someone else's house. The latter is rather important for I have £80 only in travellers' cheques left. Sorry to scratch out so much of this letter. I drank too much whisky last night and became a bore myself. Dearest Morgan, I am so pleased to see the result of the Lawrence case, though I have not seen a full report, I have had no letters for a week: they are in Kyoto, I expect, where I myself intended to be by now. I do hope all is better with you and yours; I am thinking of Rob. The weather here is very beautiful at present; yesterday I was in Shinjuku Park, so charming, looking at an exhibition of chrysanthemums, large and little; tonight I go to the Kabuki theatre. Write again soon.

Love

Joe

HART CRANE
1899 – 1932

Born Harold Crane in Garrettsville, Ohio, he left a disrupted and broken home as a young man and moved to New York and then Washington, changing his name to Hart Crane, 'Hart' being his mother's maiden name. He was a disturbed man, paranoid and hysterical, and drank too much. After his first love affair, he wrote:

> And factory sounds and factory thoughts
> Were banished from him by that larger hand
> That lay in his with the sun upon it.
> And as the bandaged knot was tightened
> The two men smiled into each others' eyes.

Hart was unhappy and promiscuous; his brief, loveless affairs were mostly with passing soldiers and sailors. He tried marriage – disastrously; his home was quarrelling and alcoholic like that of his childhood, and the marriage was soon dissolved. His personal life was wretched, but he found peace in writing. Brooklyn Bridge in New York was the inspiration for 'The Bridge' – a poem considered to be his greatest work. This poem was finished in Cuba, on the Isle of Pines, from where he wrote to his friend Waldo Frank:

[Isle of Pines]
August 19th '26

Dear Waldo: Here, too, is that bird with a note that Rimbaud speaks of as 'making you blush'. We are in the midst of the equatorial storm season; everyday, often at night, torrents engulf us, and the thunder rods jab and prospect in the caverns deep below that chain of mountains across. You can hear the very snakes rejoice, – the long shaken-out convulsions of rock and roots.

It is very pleasant to lie awake – just half awake – and listen. I have the most speechless and glorious dreams meanwhile. Sometimes words come and go, presented like a rose that yields only its light, never its composite form. Then the cocks begin to crow. I hear Mrs S begin to stir. She is the very elf of music, little wrinkled burnous wisp that can do anything and remembers so much! She reads Dante and falls to sleep, her cough has become so admirably imitated by the parrot that I often think her *[in]* two places at once.

I have made up a kind of friendship with that idiot boy, who is always on the road when I come into town for mail. He has gone so far as to answer my salutations. I was unexpected witness one day of the most astonishing spectacle; not that I was surprised. – A group of children were shrieking about in a circle. I looked toward the house and saw the boy standing mostly hid behind the wooden shutters behind the grating; his huge limp phallus waved out at them from some opening; the only other part visible was his head, in a most gleeful grin, swaying above the lower division of the blinds.

When I saw him next he was talking to a blue little kite high in the afternoon. He is rendingly beautiful at times; I have encountered him in the road, talking again tout seul and examining pebbles and cinders and marble chips through the telescope of a twice-opened tomato can. He is very shy, hilarious, – and undoubtedly idiot. I have been surprised to notice how much the other children like him.

I'm glad to know that *The Bridge* is fulfilling your utmost intuitions; for an intuition it undoubtedly was. You didn't need to tell me that *[you]* had 'seen' something that memorable evening, although I was never so sure just what it was you saw, until now. But I have always carried that peculiar look that was in your eyes for a moment there in your room, it has often recurred in my thoughts. What I should have done without your love and most distinguished understanding is hard to say, but there is no earthly benefit for which I would exchange it. It is a harmony always with the absolute direction *[I]* always seek, often miss, but sometimes gain.

Your answer to G*[orham Munson]* on his essay was much more adept than any of my critical armament. It was complete. My greatest complaint against G is (apparently) an incorrigible streak of vulgarity, arising no doubt from some distrust in experience. Sometimes it makes him personally dangerous when he doesn't intend such. Not especially par example, BUT: when I last dined with G much happened to be said about my 'extravagances' – how I spent K*[ahn]*'s money, etc. Snowshoes, African sculpture, etc. I happened to mention how useful the snowshoes had been during the storms at Patterson, etc. G recently visited the Tates and went up to my room, accompanied by Mrs Turner, who writes me, most unwittingly of the circumstances, that the main thing G quizzed her about was whether I used my snow shoes or not! Really, it *[is]* all so ridiculously small. You may think I'm wasting paper on such a silly story. But in any kind of friendship I like to have my honesty sometimes granted on my oath of it, and this is only one of many such little evidences of a real lack of perspective and innate taste on G's part. It does leak into his work, the vision of his world. He'd better memorise the last stanza of Baudelaire's famous Epilogue to the *Petits Poèmes en Prose*; as, indeed, I may sometimes tell him to do. His definition of 'knowledge' in that essay incorporates the savour of just a mind as is preoccupied with such details as I've mentioned.

Yes, I read the whole of Spengler's book. It is stupendous, – and it was perhaps a very good experience for ripening some of *The Bridge* after all. I can laugh now; but you know, alas, how little I could at the time. That book seems to have been just one more of many 'things' and circumstances that seem to have uniformly conspired in a strangely symbolical way toward the present speed of my work. Isn't it true – hasn't it been true in your experience, that beyond the acceptance of fate as a tragic action, immediately every circumstance and incident in one's life flocks toward a positive centre of action, control and beauty? I need not ask this, since there is the metaphor of the 'rotted seed of person will' or some such phrase, in your *Spain*.

I have never been able to live completely in my work before. Now it is to learn a great deal. To handle the beautiful skeins of this myth of America – to realise suddenly, as I seem to, how much of the past is living under only slightly altered forms, even in machinery and such-like, is extremely exciting. So I'm having the time of my life, just now, anyway.

By 1932 his paranoia had become a chronic hysteria. In that year, returning from Mexico, where he had moved in order to write an epic on the subject of Cortes and Montezuma, he drowned after falling, or jumping, overboard. His body was never recovered. Hart's mother died after him. Perhaps in memory of her son's poem, her ashes were scattered from Brooklyn Bridge.

FRANCIS POULENC
1899 – 1963

The composer, Francis Poulenc, was one of the most fluent and charming musicians to have emerged from France. His output was immense and his works are characterised by an ease and grace that make them immediately accessible. He was an inveterate song writer and had in the baritone Pierre Bernac a God-given collaborator. They invariably gave the first performance together (Poulenc was an accomplished pianist) and maintained a correspondence for decades. Poulenc was not outspoken about his relationships and his correspondence rarely refers to any liaisons. He was, however, a wonderful letter writer.

TO PIERRE BERNAC

Sunday [1944]

Mon petit Pierre,

A very nice Parisian refugee has kindly offered to take this letter to you, and once again, I am using you as my central distributor of news. In the first place, need I say how thirsty we all are here for news of you all, and of our dear Paris. The wildest rumours have been circulating. We were told that 100,000 had been killed in Paris alone. The improbability of this extraordinary figure was enough in itself to reassure me. We heard that the Opéra had burnt down, Les Invalides and the Gabriel buildings entirely destroyed, the Luxembourg Gardens riddled with shells, etc. Regardless of whether this was a lot of boloney or the sad truth, I naturally had to hide it all from Uncle Royer. As we have been without electricity and radio for three weeks, news has only reached us on the grapevine. Here, we feared the worst might happen, but thank God we have been spared. The Americans, arriving from Rennes, Laval, very quickly liberated our zone, but the Germans had blown up all the bridges and we feared they might put up some resistance. Enormous naval guns at Saint-Avertin were aimed at the Tranchée de Tours, Route du Mans, etc. We expected a small-scale defence of Amboise. We believed, thanks to the common sense of the Americans and the local resistance movement, that the jerries would push off by themselves, which in fact they did on Friday, the day before yesterday.

When the Americans arrived, Raymond *[Destouches]* behaved marvellously. He was fishing on the banks of the Loire when the first convoy came past, heading for Amboise. Wild with joy he hung on to one of the tanks and followed them right to the bridge of Amboise. At that point the Germans, hidden all along the avenue, let off a volley of machine-gun fire that killed three American soldiers. Protected by the tank, Raymond was unhurt. The Americans immediately aimed their tank guns at Amboise. Raymond begged the commanding officer not to fire as there were only about fifty soldiers in the town, who were likely not to be hit because they were on a lower level than the embankment, and the town itself would get the worst of it. Because of Raymond's trustworthy look, and his certificate from the English Red Cross, the commanding officer agreed not to fire and instead marshalled his convoy along the roads leading down to Nazelles. He gave a radio transmitter to Raymond, who crossed the Loire secretly in a fishing boat and went to find the Mayor of Amboise. When they had made sure that there were no more than sixty to eighty Germans in Amboise, the Americans withdrew to Pocé, with two dangerous missions to accomplish, one of which was to free Loches, also occupied by the Germans.

Such was the good work done by our young man. Tell his friends all this *in detail*, please... He will probably go back to Paris soon and will return later to fetch Uncle Papoum, deeply shaken by these events. As for me, I went through sheer anguish thinking of you all and, I must confess, equal anguish thinking of my Paris. You know my passion for that city, as much for what is beautiful in it as for its more humble rue de Belleville or rue de la Chapelle. I am suffering, too, from not being there while everything is being reorganised, not that I'm on the lookout for a job (I would refuse any offered) but to be able to make my voice heard in the way of justice, as everyone knows I am perfectly pure and independent...

I have been feeling well only for the past fortnight. Before that I suffered intermittent pains in the joints, sometimes accompanied by a temperature. Now that autumn has settled in, I feel reborn. I shall remember this year's stay here for a long time; it's only natural that in one way or another I should be punch-drunk from the events of this summer.

I have copied out the first act of *Les Mamelles*, except for the finale. The second (completely written also except for the finale), is coming along well, too. The work is far longer than I had anticipated. At least fifty minutes. I really think it is very good and that there are no holes in it. What I like about it now is that it is difficult to find the places where either the prosody or the poetic sense were so troublesome. In the text, the word Paris keeps cropping up; perhaps this, together with my nostalgia for its streets, enabled me to capture that moving tone in the midst of all the typically Apollinairian larks. Regarding the tessitura, it could not be more precisely defined, that is all I can tell you. We can go through it together with a finetooth comb, if you like.

Give my news to Marie-Blanche *[de Polignac]*, Marie-Laure *[de Noailles]*, Jacques *[Février]*, and very especially to Edouard Bourdet, Inv. 67-80, to whom I replied by the last mail and who no doubt has never received my letter...

When I think that Noizay is so totally untouched I feel almost ashamed. I hope that *Figure humaine* and *Les Mamelles* will prove a sufficient tribute from a Frenchman. The people of Noizay have been very good to me. Some of them even wanted to make me... Mayor! What a farce! Tell Marie-Blanche to cheer her up. Actually, I am sorry I could not oblige because there is nobody suitable here; but, alas, what could I possibly do for them? Try to send me some news.

I embrace you affectionately.

Fr.

Kindest regards to your dear mother.

The day the Americans arrived, I triumphantly placed my Cantata *[Figure humaine]* on the desk in the study, near my flag, at the window.

PAUL BOWLES
born 1910

The novelist and composer Paul Bowles was born in New York where he later studied music with Virgil Thompson and Aaron Copland. He was introduced to Gertrude Stein and Alice B. Toklas in Paris who advised him to visit Morocco. It clearly made a profound impression on him because he became a frequent visitor to North Africa, finally settling there in 1952. His early life, particularly in Paris, was closely bound up with the extraordinarily vital creative life of that city and his circle of friends was predominantly homosexual. His marriage to Jane did cause him considerable stress because of her bouts of mental instability, and whilst according to his friends he was not greatly interested in a vibrant erotic life, he clearly did experiment.

TO VIRGIL THOMSON

Westhampton, Massachusetts
Summer 1933

I am so very glad you are coming in October! Be sure to! I look forward to a gloomy Winter without you. Was entertained a while ago at the MacLeishes with Sessions, and that sort of thing, wrote my objections to Aaron, and sighed for you, Paris, Côte d'Azur. He replied that my impatience was charming and had got me far, 'But don't let it send you rushing back to the arms of Virgil or Abs-dabs-salaam!'

But anyway, he tried to get them to give my Apéritif Music at Yaddo and they screamed that they wouldn't consider it. Cheap, wrong, Brahms… what else. And now not your Quartet either even? What is wrong with him? I should not have minded if the objection had been that I had no métier, or that it was badly arranged, but to argue that it was cheap really is too much. Aaron soothed: 'I believe that when you perfect your technique so that you achieve a really free and complete expression of what you have to say… it will impose itself…' But I don't believe myself more than 50% of that.

I wish you were coming to Yaddo anyway. I'm going to try to get there, but of course I have no money here in this country, and not even an idea of how to get it. My father is hurt that I don't accept his invitation to live at home! I cordially invite you! And even then you won't!

Very well, it's quite all right. Still, I may have to.

What will Antheil be like in New York? I have trouble imagining him. And Sidèry playing in Peter Pan. Are you fixing it all up with Gertrude or what? I hear she considers me a fruit, and that I must be had in season. So they say she says in her Toklas autobiography.

I have been back for ten days with aunts and relatives, back in the accustomed mist of Besant, Leadbetter, Krishnamurti, Prince Mozumdar, Nirvana, Life, Omniscience, the Oneness, the partless Brahm, Blavatsky, Karessa, clouds and darkness and Karma, the Master and Truth, Truth, Truth. Everyone agreed I had had a spiritual awakening, and so did I and brought out the Koran to prove it. Later I was asked to give a little speech telling just how the revelation could come to one so young, with details of life at Eerde.

I am so completely alone here that sometimes I am at a loss to know what to do. And that for the first time in my life. I really do want to see people once in a while. Instead, I have to follow brooks to their sources and plan new four-hour walks. Utter silence, utter country. And chastity, moreover! Since Morocco, without one break. It gets on one's nerves, there's no doubt about that. And gets into one's music, but America is America.

I never told you about Porquerolles. How finally I managed to get one of the two who held out for fifty francs. Not *the* voyou, but one of two who came up to us on the quai. The next day he came to my house there and went away satisfied with a handshake. 'Le jour même j'ai pris un coup de soleil. C'était fini!' I was encouraged by those tactics and used them perfectly everywhere later: Marseille and points south.

On leur donne la main…

'Ti po'm trouver n'importe quelle nuit ici sur la place.' 'J'y conny un p'tit hotel chinois.' 'On est camarade, hein?' 'Si ti vo, j'y travaille pour toi…, je fais maquereau et je te fais le manger.' 'Je t'attends.'

[You shake hands with them…

'Any night you finding me here on the square.' 'I am knowing of a lil' Chinese hotel.' 'We friends, eh?' 'You like, I working for you…' 'I playing the pimp and buying the food.' 'I am waiting for you.']

149

JEAN GENET
1910 – 1986

Genet, an illegitimate child who never knew his parents, was brought up in a children's home until his transferral to a reformatory, for theft. He spent many years in and out of prison, where he wrote his novel Our Lady of the Flowers. *He was finally released from a life sentence a result of a campaign by the French writer Jean-Paul Sartre, who, like others, recognised the quality of Genet's writing. Other works, their common hallmark being the exploration of the issues of gender, race and class, include the plays* The Maids, The Balcony, The Blacks *and, in 1966,* The Screens – *a brave political play confronting issues of racism in the context of the Algerian War. This was staged by Jean-Louis Barrault and Madeleine Renaud's company in Paris, directed by Roger Blin, to whom Genet wrote this letter:*

April 1966

My Dear Roger

Of course I am completely ignorant when it comes to the theatre in general, but I do know enough about my own.

Whenever a judge passes a sentence, let us demand that he be prepared other than by knowledge of the criminal code. Vigils, fasting, prayer, an attempted suicide or murder, could all contribute to making the sentence he is going to pass an event so momentous – I mean a poetic event – that he, the judge, having rendered it, will be completely exhausted, on the verge of rendering his soul either unto death or madness. Bloodless, voiceless, he would take two or three years to recover. This is a great deal to ask of a judge. But what about us? We are still a long way from the poetic act. All of us – you, me, the actors – must steep ourselves for a long time in the shadows, we must work until we are utterly worn out, so that one evening we come to the brink of the final act. And we must make many mistakes, and profit from them. The fact is that we still have a long way to go, and for this play neither madness nor death seems to be the fairest sanction. And yet it is these twin goddesses that we must move in order that they may turn their attention to us. No, we are in no danger of death, nor has poetry come the way it should.

150

If I wanted what you had promised me, bright lights, it was so that each actor would finish his gestures or lines brilliantly and would rival the brightest of lights. I also wanted the house lights to be on: with the collective ass of the audience scrunched down in its seats, its immobility imposed by the acting – that was enough to make a distinction between the stage and that house, but the lights are necessary for complicity to be established. A poetic act, not a spectacle, even were it beautiful in the normal sense of the term, would have taken place. Only Maria Casarès, because of her own innate ability, performed brilliantly the last evening.

In another letter, which you have probably lost, I told you that my books, like my plays, were written against myself. You know what I mean. Among other things, this: the soldier scenes are meant to exalt – and I mean *exalt* – the Army's prime, its chief, virtue: stupidity. Real paratroopers have given me a hard-on; I've never had an erection over stage paratroopers. And if I do not succeed through the text itself to expose myself, then you have to help me. Against myself, against ourselves, whenever these performance put us on God knows what decent side into which poetry fails to penetrate.

We have to consider that we have failed. Our fault lies in having lost our nerve, collapsing like a bagpipe which deflates as it emits a few sounds that we would like to think are attractive, and in our yielding to the illusion that the finished melody was well worth the loss of precious air. By small, successive stages we have slowly but surely turned the play into something insipid. Successive stages in order to make certain we would have a success which, to my mind, is in the final analysis a failure.

Jacques Maglia said to me: 'Everything takes place as though the two of you, Blin and yourself, were proud as peacocks. Instead of a play which should stagger you when it is over, its seeming success reassures you.'

I surrendered on several occasions to Barrault's objections, and to your own. Your knowledge of the theatre threatens to make you avoid any errors of taste; my ignorance of this same profession should have led me towards them.

I am not maintaining that the *written* text of the play is of any great value, but I can assure you that I did not, for example, looked down on any of my characters – be it Sir Harold, the Gendarme, or the Paratroopers. You can be sure that I have never tried to 'understand' them, but, having created them, on paper and for the stage, I do not want to deny them. What binds me to them is something other than irony or contempt. They also help to shape me. I have never copied life – an event or a man, the Algerian war or colonisations – but life has, quite naturally, caused various images to come to life within me, or has illuminated them if they were already there – images which I have translated either by a character or an act. Pascal Monod, one of the students of the military, said to me after the last performance that the Army is not as much of a caricature as I have made it out. I did not have time to answer him that what we are dealing with here is a dream army, a dream roughly sketched out on paper and, poorly or well, brought to fruition on a stage, which might be wooden and whose flooring creaks beneath one's footsteps.

Let us come back to lighting. I'm sure you clearly understand that this way of playing with darkness, semi-darkness, and light is a recourse, delightful and chilly, which gives the spectator the time to go into raptures or to regain his composure. I wanted the ice floe, the promised land which blinds and is unremitting. What ever happened to that white, metallic material that Acquart once talked to us about and which, according to my instructions, should have constituted the very material wherein the actors moved and had their being? Will it be possible for you to use this mysterious, Mallarméan, and allegorical material, even if only for a single evening's performance?

People don't go off to wage war if they don't love it, if they don't feel themselves made for – or, if you wish, destined for – combat. The same holds true for the theatre. The actors, too much at ease on-stage, relax between their brief appearances, or, rather, crowd against one another around the blaring television in the actors' dressing room.

Certain canons read their breviaries at vespers while their minds are a thousand miles away precoccupied with God knows what, but twenty-year-old actors should not be canons. Even when she is off-stage, Maria Casarès remains in the wings, attentive or exhausted, but present: the others get the hell away as fast as they can. They could at least have the courtesy to listen to what their fellow actors are saying on-stage. By dialling some buttons they tune out the voices coming from the stage, bearing with them bravura or weariness, failure or cleverness, and they are watching television. They are listening to it. Instead of leaving the world, they bring it back, as though the stage were a place of perdition. Young actors are remarkable in that they are no sooner on-stage than they do all in their power to conceal themselves, to dissolve into a grisaille of words or movements. Can't you tell them that to glitter too brightly in their daily lives off-stage prevents a long contained brilliance from exploding and illuminating the stage? Even if they have only one line to deliver, one gesture to make, that line and gesture ought to contain whatever luminous quality each actor bears within himself which has been waiting for a long time for this magic moment: to be on-stage. Surely every actor must be encouraged to be – were it only for the duration of a single appearance, lightning-like and true – of such beauty that his disappearance into the wings will literally break the audience's heart. And that the public, though it remains under the spell of what succeeds his exit, will still miss him after he is gone.

Finally, if I am so insistent about the bright lights, both the stage and house lights, it is because I should in some way like both actors and audience to be caught up in the same illumination, and for there to be no place for them to hide, or even half-hide.

There are the few notes, my dear Roger, that the production of *The Screens* and my friendship for you compelled me to make.

J.G

PATRICK WHITE
1912 – 1990

Patrick White was one of Australia's greatest novelists, indeed with the publication of The Tree of Man *in 1955, his reputation one of the major literary figures writing in English was established. His best-known work is probably the novel,* Voss, *set in mid nineteenth-century Sydney and containing at its core a powerful exploration of a secret love affair between the explorer and scientist Voss and a young orphaned girl, Laura. His letters which often refer to his sexuality invariably reveal an acute psychological probing of the gay sensibility; this one to Gwen and David Moore, however, delivers an amusing anecdote:*

15 May 1958

We are only now on Mikonos …

For me the landscape means much more than the antiquities, as I did not have more than a very rough classical education, and besides, I am a romantic at heart. For that reason Delphi leaves the greatest impression. It is such a stupendous panorama, and the same goes for all the country between Delphi and the Ionian Sea, where we took a ferry to get to Patras. I don't think I shall ever see anything to equal what we saw in those two days, and quite untouched by tourists, officials, politicians, and all the decadent, parasitic life of Athens …

Sparta again was a wonderful landscape that one had to bow down to, though the town itself shows no apparent traces of antiquity. Just near it we clambered up a mountain in the dusk and drizzle to the Byzantine city of Mistra, with a church perched every few hundred yards. The topmost church was of particular interest as an ancestor of Manoly's, another Emanuel Lascaris, founded it. His tomb is there, and a fresco portrait from which the Turks scratched the eyes during the Occupation. The Abbess entertained us with ouzo in a very stovey little room, and sold us embroidery when the heat and drink had broken down our resistance. (Very beautiful embroidery, too.)

… A very emotional situation has just blown up on the waterfront at Mikonos as the result of a lattice erected by two Americans to hide the goings-on in an old house they rent, and which they run as a bar. The

Prefect of the Cyclades arrived the last day of our visit, and proposed to ban the lattice as something that spoils the uniformity of the waterfront. One of the Americans has now rushed to Athens to enlist the sympathies of a Minister, and thus save the lattice. The Americans claim they are being persecuted (probably rightly) as foreigners, while the Islanders claim (rightly also, I should think) that their bar is a homosexual brothel and that the proprietors are seducing all the boys, and even the husbands on the Island! The delightful part is that, in their rage, the Islanders are practically accusing America of introducing homosexuality *into Greece*, whereas, if they want to go no farther back in history than today, the Abbot of a monastery on the far side of the Island is keeping a harem of twenty boy-orphans! (We met him while we were there, a crafty piece of work with his hair done up in a net, but all he offered us was a piece of Turkish delight.) I don't know what will come of the Lattice of Mikonos. It is a lovely plot, I think and might well end up in the fall of governments, and diplomatic incidents, for the uncle of one of the Americans is said to control Aid-to-Greece.

I have wasted a lot of time on that, and must now say something about Delos, which we visited from Mikonos, and which was a perfect idyll. A long rocky barren island covered with yellow grass and thistles, but at the same time masses of pink convolvulus, purple statice, yellow sea-poppies and the common field red, as well as a little flower resembling the gentian. The air full of a sound of what could have been deafening larks. Cisterns full of green water and enormous green, coupling frogs. Crimson dragonflies above the water, intent on the same game. And all through it, the remains of what must have been a great city, columns, temples, mosaics (fabulously beautiful ones that one wants at once for a house of one's own), with down, by the sea, propped up against stones, the marble torso of a giant Apollo, worn down by the weather to a texture of cuttlefish. We came back to Mikonos, suitably pricked by thistles and burnt by the sun, over a classic sea.

PIER PAOLO PASOLINI
1922 – 1975

One of the great figures in the artistic life of Italy in the middle of this century, Pasolini was a genuine Renaissance man, a poet, critic, film maker. His homosexuality was a constant preoccupation, as he reveals in this letter to his confidante of the time, Silvana Mauri.

Rome

10 February 1950

Dearest Silvana

I had decided to write to you again this morning because I was sorry about my last letter, which was a little too full of despair; I hope you have forgiven me. Today for no reason I was less oppressed, I had a little bit less unhappiness. Now it is already evening and I am here with your letter before my eyes. You know I am living near the ghetto a couple of steps from Cola di Rienzo's church; do you remember? I have gone over again, two or three times, our walk in '47 and even if I have not found once more that sky and that air – from the tremendous grey of the ghetto to the white of San Pietro in Montecitorio; the Jewish woman sitting beside a chain against the dark doorway; the storm with its smell of resin and then via Giulia and the Farnese Palace, that Farnese Palace which will never be repeated again as if the light after the storm had sculptured it in a veil – I was amazed and consoled.

Even now my head is buzzing with the cries in the Campo dei Fiori while the rain stopped. But this warmth which floods me like a moment of repose I owe to your letter; it is here soiled with lipstick and cream, from the carnival at Versuta and the flowers in Piazza di Spagna. In those days in '47 my descent which became a precipice after Lerici began; I canno`Ωt yet manage to pass judgement on myself not even, as would be easy, to give a negative judgement, but I think it was inevitable. You ask me to speak to you truthfully and with a sense of shame; I shall do so, Silvana, but when we talk, if it is possible to talk with a sense of shame in a case like mine: perhaps I have partly done it in my poetry. Now since I have been in Rome I just have to sit at my

156

typewriter for me to tremble and not know even what to think; the words seem to have lost their meaning. I can only tell you that the ambiguous life – as you rightly say – which I led in Casarsa I shall continue to lead in Rome. And if you think about the etymology of ambiguous you will see that someone who leads a double existence can only be ambiguous.

For this reason I sometimes – and lately often – am cold, 'nasty', my words 'hurt'. It is not a 'maudit' attitude but the obsessive need not to deceive others, to come out with what I *also* am. I apparently did not have a religious or moralistic education or past but for long years I was what is called the consolation of my parents, a model son, an ideal scholar... This tradition of mine of honesty and uprightness – which had no name or faith but which was rooted in me with the anonymous profundity of something natural – for long prevented me from accepting the verdict. You must imagine my case as being a little like that of Fabio without psychiatrists, priests, treatments and symptoms and crises, but that – as was the case with Fabio – I distanced myself, absented myself. I do not know if there are any longer ordinary measures for judging me or if one should not rather have recourse to the exceptional ones adopted for sick persons. My apparent health, my equilibrium, my unnatural resistance, can be deceptive... But I see that I am looking for justifications once again... Forgive me – I only wanted to say that it is not possible for me nor will it ever be possible to speak of myself with shame: and instead it will be necessary often to stand in the pillory because I do not want to deceive anyone – as basically I deceived you and other friends who talk about an old Pier Paolo or of a Pier Paolo who has to be a new self. I do not know what to understand by hypocrisy but now I am in terror of it. Enough half-words – the scandal has to be faced, I think St Paul said... I think in this connection that I want to live in Rome precisely because here I shall be neither an old nor a new Pier Paolo. Those who like me have been fated not to love according to the rules end up by overvaluing the question of love. A normal person can resign himself – that terrible word – to chastity, to lost opportunities; but in me the difficulty in loving has made the need for love obsessive: the function made the organ hypertrophic when, as an adolescent, love seemed to me an unattainable chimera: then when with experience the function had resumed its proper proportions and the chimera had been deconsecrated to the point of being the most miserable daily matter, the evil was already inoculated, chronic and incurable. I found myself with an enormous mental organ for a function which by now is so negligible that only yesterday with all my misfortunes and my fits of remorse – there was an uncontainable despair for a boy sitting on a low wall and left behind for all time and in all places by the tram as it went along. As you see I am talking to you with extreme sincerity and I do not know with how much shame. Here in Rome I can find more easily than elsewhere the way of living ambiguously, do you understand? and at the same time the way of being entirely sincere, of not deceiving anyone as I would end up doing in Milan: perhaps I am telling you this because I am discouraged and place you by yourself on the pedestal of someone who is able to understand and feel for me: but the fact is that up to now I have not found anyone as sincere as I would wish. The sexual life others had always made me ashamed of mine: is the wrong all on my side? It seems impossible to me. Understand me, Silvana, what I have most at heart is to be clear to myself and to others – with a clarity that has no half measures, is ferocious. It is the only way to make me forgive that terrifyingly honest and good boy which someone in me continues to be. But about all this – which will continue to be a little obscure to you because it is said too confusedly and rapidly – we will be able to talk in a more leisurely way. So I think I shall stay in Rome – this new Casarsa – all the more since I have no intention either of knowing or meeting literary people, persons who have always terrified me because they always ask for opinions while I have none. I intend to work and to love, both desperately. But then you will ask if what has happened to me – punishment, as you rightly call it – has been of no use to me. Yes, it has been of use but not to change me and even less to redeem me; but it was of use to me to understand that I had touched bottom, that the experience had been exhausted and I could begin from the beginning but without repeating the same mistakes; I have liberated myself from my iniquitous and fossil perversion, now I feel lighter and my libido is a cross, no longer a weight that drags me down to the depths.

I have re-read what I have written to you up to now and am very unhappy with it; perhaps you will find it a little chilling again like the letter after Lerici, but bear in mind that then my descent into distrust, incredulity, disgust was beginning, while now I am rising up again, or at least so I hope. You will be able to guess how much of the pathological and febrile lies in my words, what traces my despair of these days has left there. Other phrases you must not take at their face value. For example, 'Rome, this new Casarsa' is a phrase which mustn't make you throw up your hands even if it is rather nasty; there is also a good Casarsa and it is the latter I wish to regain. This latest crisis in my life, an external crisis, which is the trace of that internal one which I postponed from day to day, has, I hope, re-established a certain equilibrium. There are moments when life is open like a fan, you see everything in it, and then it is fragile, insecure and too vast. In my statements and in my confessions try to catch a glimpse of this totality. My future life will certainly not be that of a university professor; by now I bear the mark of Rimbaud, or Campana and also of Wilde, whether I want it or not, whether others accept it or not. It is something uncomfortable, annoying and inadmissible, but that is how it is; and I, like you, do not give in. From certain of your words ('...among things which have caused you pain if they really caused you pain') I am to understand that you too, like many others, suspect some aestheticism and some complacency in my case. But you are wrong, you are absolutely wrong in this. I have suffered what can be suffered, I have never accepted my sin, I have never come to terms with my nature and have not even become used to it I was born to be calm, balanced and natural; my homosexuality was something additional, was outside, had nothing to do with me. I always saw it alongside me like an enemy, I never felt it within me. Only in this last year I let myself go to some extent; but I was exhausted, my family situation was disastrous, my father raged and was nasty to a sickening degree, my poor communism had made me hated, as one hates a monster, by a whole community, a literary failure also loomed; and then the search for an immediate pleasure, a pleasure to die in, was the only escape. I have been punished for it without pity. But this too we shall talk about or else I shall write to you about it more calmly, now I have too many things to say to you; I shall add right away in this connection a detail: it was at Belluno when I was three and a half (my brother was not yet born) that I felt for the first time that most sweet and violent attraction which then remained within me – always the same, blind and sinister like a fossil.

It did not yet have a name but was so strong and irresistible that I had to invent one myself: it was 'teta veleta' and I write it for you trembling, so much does this terrible name invented by a child of three in love with a boy of thirteen frighten me – this name which belongs to the fetish, the primordial, the disgusting and the affectionate. From then on it is a long story which I leave it to you to imagine if you can. Getting on for nineteen, a little before we met, I had a crisis which was within a hair's breadth of being identical with Fabio's; but instead it resolved itself in a neurosis which was not very serious, in a state of exhaustion, in an obsessive thought of suicide (which often comes over me still) and then in recovery. In '42 in Bologna, do you remember? I was as strong as a horse by then and sound as a tree. But it was a flourishing state that was not to last.

You have been something special to me and different from all the rest; so exceptional that I can find no explanation for it – not even one of those spectral explanations which are so concrete, which we seize on in our internal monologue: in our astute manoeuvering of our thought. From the time when you opened the door to me in Bologna, a few days after I met Fabio, and appeared to me in the shape of a 'thirteenth-century madonna' (I think I said this to you) at the Malga Troi, in Milan, after the war, at Bompiani's, in Versuta, in Rome, you have always been for me the woman I could have loved, the only one who led me to understand what a woman is, and the only one who up to a certain point I have loved. You know what that point is: but now I have to tell you that sometimes I know neither how nor when I passed it timidly, madly, but I did pass it. If you want to think of a similar situation think of 'Strait is the gate'; but I have never said anything to you about my tender feelings, because I did not trust myself. Don't make me add any more, understand me. In my last letter I wrote that you were the only one among my friends in whom I was able to confide; and this simply because you are the only one I truly love to the point of sacrifice. For you, to be of help or a comfort to you, I would do anything without the least shadow of indecision or of selfishness.

Now here, your letter if I look at it, moves me ferociously, I feel tears in my eyes; I think of what I have lost, at the waste of my life into which I have been unable to welcome you.

I cannot go on with this letter; the other things I have to say to you I shall write tomorrow. I could continue only if I could let myself go, but I cannot, I have to melt so much ice within me. Forgive me if I have written you another nasty letter but if I could write nicely, with all the niceness of another time, then this letter would not have been necessary. I am furious with myself and my impotence, while I would like to tell you of all my tenderness and my affection.

A hug, Pier Paolo

Pasolini's death remains a mystery; was he murdered by a violent rent-boy or was there a political motive?

NEIL BARTLETT
born 1958

The playwright and actor Neil Bartlett wrote a dramatic tribute to Oscar Wilde, Who was that man? *drawing on his life and works. At the end of the work he writes two letters to Oscar Wilde, a bitter reflection viewed back through the years:*

Dear Oscar,

I know it's a bad habit to write late at night, especially when you're drunk, but still.

When I went to Paris to put the flowers on your grave, I made the gesture out of real love and respect. I got dressed up. I made myself just as handsome as I could, so handsome that the men would look at me on the journey. I made a point of buying the roses from the florist in the Burlington Arcade (remember?) and then when I got to Paris I walked straight to the grave and laid them down with all the other flowers looking just as strong as I could, stood there with a smile on my face and I didn't cry once. I smoked a whole cigarette for you and then turned and went. And then I came back to London and started writing. Darling, it's all for you. We're doing all this for you. I wish you could be here to see us. The streets are not all that different – you wouldn't get lost – but we are very different these days. Can you imagine, tonight I walked down the Strand with my lover, and we talked about which pub we would go and drink in; we have a choice of places to go now, and the chances are that when we get there no one will know us. And then he put his arm round my shoulder. I suppose it's gestures like that, public and unremarkable, that you could never enjoy. I can't make it up to you, and it doesn't justify what they did to you, but I wanted to tell you nevertheless. I think you didn't know things were going to change, and that really you weren't trying to change anything. You weren't thinking about us. The weight of a lover's arm on your shoulder is not a sensation you can ever enjoy now, nothing can ever be worth what was done to you, nothing can change that, but oh almost it does. We're walking your streets.

> We're doing it all for you. It's all for you,
> Love,

Oscar, you fat bitch,

Last night I dreamed your hand was on my face. You were there in the bed, big and fat like I've been told you were, lying in bed smoking and taking up all the room. It was quite funny at first. I tried to ignore you. I tried to get back to sleep, but I was uneasy about sleeping. I thought you might be watching. Sometimes, half-asleep, I'd roll over and knock against your body, our skins would rub together, and then I'd feel your hand on my face. I'd wake up and try to apologize. You said nothing but kept on smoking. I noticed that I didn't recognize either the smell or the brand of your cigarettes. I suppose you didn't have the same kind of cigarettes then. So I got up and put on the light and fetched an ashtray and waited for you to talk. I realized that I had no idea what your voice would sound like. Once the light was on I wasn't embarrassed, really, by your body. You didn't try to cover yourself. You are old, and fat, and white, and you sweat slightly. You're an old queen; you are quite beyond being embarrassed by a younger man, quite capable of taking in the details of my body (I had half an erection swinging when I went to get the ashtray from the kitchen) without desire or inhibition. So I came back into the bed and sat close. I thought, having read about you that you might want to run your fingers through my hair. I know I'm not blonde, and that I don't look like a boy any more now that I've made myself look like a man, but I still thought that you might want to touch me. I thought you might want something from me. I thought I might have something to give you. I leaned against your shoulder and waited.

I wanted you to talk; I would have listened to anything you might have said. I would have held you if you'd wanted me to. I would have talked or listened all night. After all, I've done that for a lot of other men. I would have done anything; masturbated in front of you, or let you do anything you wanted.

And you said nothing, you didn't even look at me half the time. You smoked. Your eyes were dead, your fat white flesh was sweating slightly and quite dead. You used your right hand to bring your cigarette to your mouth with an absolute economy of effort. I supposed that they had finally managed to kill you. To reduce you to this. I couldn't talk, couldn't even ask you for a cigarette (that would have been something for me, you see, to smoke one of your cigarettes, to wake up with that taste in my mouth). I couldn't say what I wanted to say. I don't pity you. I don't even want to ask your advice, just to hear your stories; I'll work out what they might mean to me. Please, say anything at all to me, and I can use it. You old queen, you've got your hand on my face, I can't talk now.

Love,

PETER TATCHELL
born 1952

At the end of 1994, the leadership of the Anglican Church was refusing to discuss homosexual issues. Since polite lobbying had failed, Outrage!, the gay pressure group, felt that more challenging tactics were necessary. In November 1994, ten bishops were named and urged to 'Tell The Truth' about their sexuality. Within a fortnight, senior church leaders began serious discussions with lesbian and gay organisations for the first time. Not long after the world conference of Anglican leaders called on the Church to rethink its policy on homosexuality, and the Archbishop of Canterbury declared that lesbians and gays are 'made in the image and likeness of God' and that society must 'reject homophobia'. The following letter was sent by Peter Tatchell of Outrage! to the Bishop of London, the Rt Rev. David Hope:

London
30 December 1994

I have taken the trouble to hand deliver this letter to you because it is for your eyes only. I wanted to save you any embarrassment in the event of it being opened and read by any of your assistants.

As you are no doubt aware, it is widely understood by many lesbians and gay men, religious affairs correspondents and clergy and administrators of the Church of England that you are gay.

Although OutRage! has been passed a lot of detailed information about your personal life, which would have enabled us to confidently name you at Synod on 30 November, we chose not to do so.

The reason is this: we believe that you are, or can be, a person of honesty and courage. You have the potential to play a very special rôle, both morally and historically. It is our sincere hope that you will find the inner strength and conviction to realize the importance of *voluntarily* coming out as gay and of speaking out in defence of lesbian and gay human rights.

I understand that this will not be an easy decision for you. But since when has bearing witness for truth and justice ever been easy for anyone living in a society based on dishonesty and injustice?

Regrettably, it is often only by taking the hard option, rather than the easy one, that truth and justice can be secured.

I am aware that you have shown private kindness and understanding to gay clergy in your diocese. However, the time for purely private acts of goodness is past. What is now necessary are public acts of moral leadership which challenge the homophobia blighting the lives of homosexual men and women.

Let me assure you that any discomfort you may suffer as a consequence of coming out and speaking out will be far outweighed by the positive changes that your actions will help bring about. You must balance your own relatively minor personal hardship against the far greater hardship endured by the millions of lesbian and gay people who are victimized by our homophobic society, often with the collusion of the Church. Your coming out and speaking out can make a really important difference to their lives.

You can give many vulnerable, suffering lesbian and gay people (especially lesbian and gay Christians) reassurance, confidence and hope.

You can give the campaign for lesbian and gay human rights new credibility and influence, which will eventually contribute to legislative changes preventing homosexuals from being sacked from their jobs, banned from membership of the Armed Forces, refused political asylum, arrested for consenting relations if they are under 18, denied custody of their children by the courts, and prevented from marrying the person they love.

By coming out and speaking out, you can also ensure that the Church of England begins to make a fundamental break with its past and present homophobia. Your openness and commitment to our human rights could help precipitate a dramatic change in Anglican attitudes and policies: an end to the sacking of gay clergy, the overturning of the Children's Society's ban on gay foster carers, and the axing of Anglican support for organisations attempting to brainwash homosexuals and make them straight.

It is within your personal power to be an agent for the liberation of lesbian and gay people – or you can continue to remain silent and to passively collude with our victimisation. The choice is yours.

You are, however, not alone. There are 10 other Bishops we named at Synod, plus five others we did not name (for various reasons). After our naming of the Bishops, two of them (John Saterthwaite and John Nicholls) issued ambiguous statements which some people have interpreted as a de facto coming out. Furthermore, Derek Rawcliffe (Hon. Assistant Bishop, Ripon) has been semi-open for over a year.

The Bishop of Wakefield has recently emphasised that having a homosexual orientation is not sinful and is no bar to holding high office in the Church of England. It would therefore seem unproblematic for you and others to be open about being gay by orientation.

If you are concerned about acting alone, perhaps you could consult with the other Bishops and arrange for several of you to issue a joint declaration of your gay orientation and of your collective commitment to a revision of Anglican policy and the repeal of anti-gay laws. That way you could give each other support and solidarity, and protect yourselves against being picked off one-by-one.

In making your decision, I ask you to seriously contemplate the terrible suffering that many (not all) lesbian and gay people experience because of homophobic prejudice. Think of the following individuals who came to OutRage! in desperation:

• The 13-year-old teenager who was being beaten by his parents after they discovered he was gay.

• The Iranian lesbian who was refused political asylum and deported back to Iran and has since disappeared (presumably executed).

• The employee who was sacked from his job when he complained about being harassed because of his homosexuality.

• The gay man who was imprisoned for seven years on sexual assault charges which were almost certainly trumped up by local gangsters who were blackmailing him.

• The lovers who cannot live together because one is American and has been refused residence rights in the UK, despite a long-standing relationship with his male partner.

• The gay man nearly battered to death who, when he reported the attack to the police, was abused and threatened with arrest.

• The lesbian who had her child taken from her by the courts because the judge deemed that her lesbianism rendered her unfit to care for her own son.

It is for the sake of these people, and the many others who suffer similar homophobic victimisation, that I ask you to be honest and brave. Do not do it for me or for OutRage! Please, do it for *them*.

There are very few people who are presented with an opportunity to do something with their lives that can be of profound social importance. You have such an opportunity.

No Bishop has ever come out fully and publicly. No Anglican leader has ever crusaded for lesbian and gay human rights. If you take this step, you will be doing something uniquely honourable and worthwhile.

I implore you, do not walk by on the other side of the street while lesbian and gay people are suffering. Come over to our side of the street and support us in our struggle for the dignity and human rights which are the entitlement of all men and women.

You are in my thoughts. May you have the strength and courage to do what it is right and necessary.

> Yours sincerely,
> Peter Tatchell

Since receiving the letter the Bishop has admitted that his sexuality is 'ambiguous' but, more encouragingly, he has been promoted to Archbishop of York. Outrage!'s initial plan for the Church to accept and support gay men and women appears to have worked. Whatever one's views of 'outing', Outrage! achieved more in the few months late in 1994 than many other pressure groups have achieved in years.

ARMISTEAD MAUPIN
(born 1944)

Although all the other letters in this book are from real people, we felt that the following fictional one, Michael 'Mouse' Tolliver's 'Letter to Mama' from Armistead Maupin's More Tales of the City, *was both relevant and irresistible.*

Dear Mama,

I'm sorry it's taken me so long to write. Every time I try to write to you and Papa I realize I'm not saying the things that are in my heart. That would be OK, if I loved you any less than I do, but you are still my parents and I am still your child.

I have friends who think I'm foolish to write this letter. I hope they're wrong. I hope their doubts are based on parents who loved and trusted them less than mine do. I hope especially that you'll see this as an act of love on my part, a sign of my continuing need to share my life with you.

I wouldn't have written, I guess, if you hadn't told me about your involvement in the Save Our Children campaign. That, more than anything, made it clear that my responsibility was to tell you the truth, that your own child is homosexual, and that I never needed saving from anything except the cruel and ignorant piety of people like Anita Bryant.

I'm sorry, Mama. Not for what I am, but for how you must feel at this moment. I know what that feeling is, for I felt it for most of my life. Revulsion, shame, disbelief – rejection through fear of something I knew, even as a child, was as basic to my nature as the color of my eyes.

No, Mama, I wasn't 'recruited'. No seasoned homosexual ever served as my mentor. But you know what? I wish someone had. I wish someone older than me and wiser than the people in Orlando had taken me aside and said, 'You're all right, kid. You can grow up to be a doctor or a teacher just like anyone else. You're not crazy or sick or evil. You can succeed and be happy and find peace with friends – all kinds of friends – who don't give a damn *who* you go to bed with. Most of all, though, you can love and be loved, without hating yourself for it.'

But no one ever said that to me, Mama. I had to find it out on my own, with the help of the city that has become my home. I know this may be hard for you to believe, but San Francisco is full of men and women, both straight and gay, who don't consider sexuality in measuring the worth of another human being. These aren't radicals and weirdos, Mama. They are shop clerks and bankers and little old ladies and people who nod and smile to you when you meet them on the bus. Their attitude is neither patronising nor pitying. And their message is simple: Yes, you are a person. Yes, I like you. Yes, it's alright for you to like me too.

I know what you're thinking now. You're asking yourself: What did we do wrong? How did we let this happen? Which one of us made him that way?

I can't answer that, Mama. In the long run, I guess I really don't care. All I know is this: if you and Papa are responsible for the way I am, then I thank you with all my heart, for it's the light and the joy of my life.

I know I can't tell you what it is to be gay. But I can tell you what it's not.

It's not hiding behind words, Mama. Like family and decency and Christianity. It's not fearing your body, or the pleasures that God made for it. It's not judging your neighbor, except when he's crass or unkind.

Being gay has taught me tolerance, compassion and humility. It has shown me the limitless possibilities of living. It has given me people whose passion and kindness and sensibility have provided a constant source of strength.

It has brought me into the family of man, Mama, and I like it here. I *like* it.

There's not much else I can say, except that I'm the same Michael you've always known. You just know me better now. I have never consciously done anything to hurt you. I never will.

Please don't feel you have to answer this right away. It's enough for me to know that I no longer have to lie to the people who taught me to value the truth.

Mary Ann sends her love.

Everything is fine at 28, Barbary Lane.

> Your loving son,
> Michael

SOURCES AND BIBLIOGRAPHY

The editors and publishers wish to thank those who gave their permission to use extracts from the stated works. Acknowledgements are as follows:

Emperor Hadrian letter B.W. Henderson, *The Life and Principate of Hadrian*, Methuen & Co Ltd, 1923

Alexius Comnenus letter J. Boswell, *Christianity, Social Tolerance and Homosexuality*, University of Chicago Press, 1980

Pope Honorius III letter J. Boswell, *Christianity, Social Tolerance and Homosexuality*, University of Chicago Press, 1980

Edward II letters ed H. Johnstone, *The Letters of Edward, Prince of Wales, 1304–1305*, The Roxburghe Club, Cambridge University Press, 1931 (Second letter transl B. Homewood)

Leonardo da Vinci letter *The Literary Works of Leonardo da Vinci*, Phaidon, 1970

Erasmus letters F.M. Nichols, *Epistles of Erasmus*, Longmans, Green & Co, 1901

Michelangelo letters G. Bull, *Michelangelo, Life, Letters & Poetry*, Oxford University Press, 1987

Bazzi letter R.H. Hobart Cust, *Giovanni Antonio Bazzi*, John Murray, 1906

Aretino letter R.H. Hobart Cust, *Giovanni Antonio Bazzi*, John Murray, 1906

Sidney letters Pierce, *The Correspondence of Sir Philip Sidney & Hubert Languet*, William Pickering, London, 1845

Anthony and Francis Bacon letters D. du Maurier, *Golden Lads*, Victor Gollancz Ltd, 1973

Francis Bacon letters J. Spedding, *The Letters and Life of Francis Bacon*, Vol VII, Longmans, Green, Reader and Dyer, 1874

King James I letters M. Sanders, *Intimate Letters of England's Kings*, Museum Press Ltd, 1959

John Winthrop letter J. Goldberg, *Queering the Renaissance*, Duke University Press, 1994

Philippe, duc d'Orléans, Princess Henrietta, Princess Charlotte letters H. Stokes, *Prince of Pleasure*, Herbert Jenkins Ltd 1912

Henderson, *A Lady of the Old Régime,* George Bell & Sons, 1909

Correa Netto letters K. Gerard & G. Hekina, *The Pursuit of Sodomy,* Harrington Park Press, 1988

Frederick the Great and Voltaire letters R. Aldington, *Letters of Voltaire & Frederick the Great,* 1927

Gray letter Matthison and R. & W.A. Bortow, *Gray's Letters & Poems,* W.A. Bortow & Co, Richmond, Virginia, 1821

Walpole letter Mrs Paget Tonybee, *Walpole Letters,* Vol I & IV, The Clarendon Press, 1803

Winckelmann letter J.J. Winckelmann *Letter to Count Bruhl, 1771*

Byron letters Prothero, *The Works of Lord Byron,* John Murray, 1898, *Private Correspondence of Lord Byron,* John Murray, 1824

Withers/Hammond letters ed M. Duberman, *Hidden from History,* Penguin Books, USA, 1989

Fitzgerald letters ed W.A. Wright, *Letters and Literary Remains of Edward Fitzgerald,* MacMillan & Co, 1889

Chopin letter ed Bronislaw Edward Sydow, transl A Headley, *Selected Correspondence of Fryderick Chopin,* Heinemann, 1962

Melville letter M. Minnigrode, *Some Personal Letters of Herman Melville,* Edmond Byrne Hackett, 1922

Whitman letter ed E. H. Miller, *Walt Whitman The Correspondence* Vol II (1868-1875), New York University Press, 1961

Addington Symonds letters *The Letters of John Addington Symonds,* Vol III, Wayne State University Press, 1969

Tchaikovsky letter ed A. Orlova, transl R.M. Davison, *Tchaikovsky. A Self-Portrait,* Oxford University Press, 1990

Sullivan letter A. Lawrence, *Sir Arthur Sullivan,* James Bowden, 1899

Henry James letters P. Lubbock, *The Letters of Henry James,* Vol II, Macmillan & Co Ltd, 1920

Wilde letter ed R. Hart Davies, *Selected Letters of Oscar Wilde,* 1979, reprinted by permission of Oxford University Press and Merlin Holland

Housman letter *Letters from A.E. Housman to E.M. Blakeney,* Private Press, Winchester, 1941

Casement letter P. Singleton-Gates, *The Black Diaries,* Olympia Press, 1959

Proust letters ed P. Kolb *Marcel Proust. Selected Letters* Vol III, HarperCollins 1992

Gide letter ed P. Kolb *Marcel Proust. Selected Letters* Vol III,
HarperCollins, 1992

E.M. Forster letter ed M. Largo and P. N. Furbank *Selected Letters of
E.M. Forster*, Collins, 1988

Nicolson letters ed N. Nicolson *Vita and Harold*, Weidenfeld &
Nicolson, 1992

Brooke letter Berg Berg Collection, New York

T.E. Lawrence letter D. Garnett, *Letters of T.E. Lawrence*, Jonathan
Cape, 1938

Cocteau letter *Francis Poulenc. Selected Correspondence* 1915-1963,
Gollancz, 1991

Nijinsky letter *The Diary of Vaslav Nijinsky*, Quartet Books, 1991

Ackerley letters by permission of David Higham Associates

Crane letter ed B. Weber, *The Letters of Hart Crane*, University of
California Press, 1963

Poulenc letter *Francis Poulenc. Selected Correspondence* 1915-1963,
Gollancz, 1991

Bowles letter ed J. Miller, *In Touch. The Letters of Paul Bowles*,
HarperCollins, 1993

Genet letter J. Genet, *Reflections on the Theatre*, Faber & Faber, 1972

Pasolini letter ed N. Naldini, transl S. Hood, *The Letters of Pier Paolo
Pasolini* Vol I 1940-1954, Quartet Books, 1992

Bartlett letter N. Bartlett *Who was that man? A present for Mr Oscar
Wilde*, Serpent's Tail, 1990

Tatchell letter MS Peter Tatchell

Letter to Mama A. Maupin, *More Tales of the City*, The Chronicle
Publishing Company, 1980

White letter D. Marr, *Patrick White. A Life* Jonathan Cape, 1991

The editors and the publishers apologise if any person or estate has
been overlooked in these acknowledgements. They would be grateful
to be informed if any copyright notice has been omitted, or if there
have been any changes of ownership or location concerning letters
quoted.